Within View, Within Reach

Within View, Within Reach

Navigating the
College-Bound Journey

Samuel Stone Press
Graham, North Carolina

Within View, Within Reach
Navigating the College-bound Journey
by Robyn S. Hadley
Copyright © 2010 by Robyn S. Hadley. All Rights Reserved

ISBN: 978-0-9842425-2-8

Order from www.withinviewwithinreach.com

Cover Design by JamesG@IndyGraphics.com
Cover Photo: Purestock/Jupiterimages
Back Cover Photo by Dan Sears, the University of North Carolina at Chapel Hill

Publisher's Cataloging-in-Publication
(Provided by Quality Books, Inc.)

Hadley, Robyn S.
Within view, within reach : successfully navigating the college-bound journey / by Robyn S. Hadley.
    p. cm.
    LCCN 2010932950
    ISBN-13: 978-0-9842425-2-8 / ISBN-10: 0-9842425-2-X
    ISBN-13: 978-0-9842425-3-5/ISBN-10: 0-9842425-3-8 (e-book)

    1. Universities and colleges--Admission. 2. College choice. 3. Parent and adult child. I. Title.

LB2351.H33 2010   378.1'61   QBI10-600147

For Mom

Contents

1   Within View, Within Reach   8

2   Believing "Yes, I Can!"   15

3   Tackling the Task as a Team   23

4   Making the Grade   38

5   Finding the Right Fit   58

6   Checking Them Out   81

7   Counting the Costs   98

8   Applying to Make it Happen   111

9   Finding the Resources   130

10   Sending Them on Their Way   151

Appendices for Chapter 5   171

Appendices for Chapter 7   179

Appendices for Chapter 9   182

Appendices for Chapter 10   184

1

Within View, Within Reach

Imagine a classroom filled with tables and chairs. On one side of the room is an interior door, and on the other side of the room is a door leading to the outside. If you enter the dark room using the interior door late at night and you attempt to walk across that room to the outside door, the journey could be very hazardous. On that journey, you will likely run into tables and chairs. You may stumble, and you may get hurt. And you may get so frustrated and discouraged that you quit the journey altogether.

But what could you do to make that journey remarkably different? Turn on the lights! Once you turn on the lights, the obstacles do not magically disappear. The tables and chairs are still there.

The distance of the journey is still the same. But with the light, you can see the possible obstacles and decide how to navigate safely and effectively to reach your destination. Once the lights are on, you may see ten different paths to make your way across the room to the outside door.

The college-bound journey for you and your child may be very similar. The interior door represents where you and your child are now. The other door leading to the outside represents entry to your child's college of choice. The journey from "point A" to "point B" may be filled with several obstacles. And if you attempt to make that journey in the pitch dark, without sufficient guidance or experience lighting the way, you may get frustrated and even incur a few bumps and bruises. But worst of all, you and your child may get so discouraged that you give up on the college-bound journey altogether.

Turn on the Light

The purpose of this book is to be a source of information and insight to guide you and your child on the college-bound journey. In the following chapters, I will shed light on potential obstacles and help you see the right path toward the best college choice for your child. Each chapter will focus on a particular area where common obstacles in the college-going process are found from getting your child to simply talk about college to getting him ready and on campus for the first day of class. As new light is shed, you may discover that what seemed a good choice for your child is not necessarily the best choice, or what seemed a slim chance is a real possibility.

This book may not give you all the right answers, but I do hope it will help you know the right questions you need to ask. The college-going process can be overwhelming for any family but especially if you have never made this journey before. My goal is to help you gather the information and resources you need to determine the best steps and options for you and your child to consider and ultimately execute.

Chapter Overviews

In chapter two, we begin by addressing all the nay-sayers you may encounter on this journey. There may be voices in your own home that say, "There's no way we can afford this" or those who think your child is reaching too high. In chapter three, we talk about getting your child and others on board with the journey and examining who needs to be involved in the process.

Of course, grades do matter. So in chapter four, we address what colleges are looking for in a "good student" and how your child can prepare. This chapter also includes additional ideas that I have found give children an "extra edge" in preparing for the transition to college. But before you even apply to a college, you need to make sure the "right ones" are getting your attention. There are a lot of colleges out there, and it can be overwhelming to find the best college choice where your child will thrive. So, in chapter five, we will discuss what to consider in finding the right fit for your child's needs and aspirations.

So often we think of the college-bound journey in terms of colleges sizing up the student, but the college-going process is equally about students and families sizing up colleges and universities as well. In chapter six, we explore college tours and other ways to investigate if a particular college is the right investment and fit for your child and you.

The cost of a college education is often the biggest obstacle that most families fear. In chapter seven, we discuss what to expect financially, revealing hidden costs and even setting budgets that will help your child get to college and stay there to complete his degree. Once you and your child have determined the right fit, in chapter eight we look at how to approach the college application process to best present or introduce your child to the schools of choice. And then, in chapter nine, we look specifically at how to obtain the needed resources, including scholarships and financial aid, to make your child's educational dreams a reality.

Lastly, in chapter ten, we discuss how to prepare your family and your student for the long-awaited day when you send him on his way to college.

Bright Ideas

To make this book an even more helpful resource, **throughout each chapter look for a light bulb icon to highlight helpful points and ideas you can put into action.** These "bright ideas" are specific action points that shed light on helpful steps for you and your child as you move along the college-bound journey. At the end of each chapter, you can find a checklist summarizing all the "bright ideas" as another quick reference guide.

For many families, parents and children alike, the college-bound journey can be overwhelming and even a bit frightening. And if you are like me, things are always more scary in the dark! Remember as a child seeing the cartoons where the character is scared of the huge monster in the corner of the room? But when the light is turned on, he realizes that the huge monster was only a small mouse which simply projected a large and frightening shadow.

Many of the obstacles we most fear about college are not as big and scary as they may initially seem. Once we "turn on the light," we can see what we are really dealing with and how we can address what needs to be done. Granted, there are times where the light helps us realize what is not realistic – or more appropriately – is not the best fit. But even more often, the light helps us see what is possible and what is clearly within view and within reach.

Conceive it.

Believe it.

Achieve it.

These are the three critical steps on the college-bound journey. Together, with this book as your guide, I hope you and your child will be able to SEE or CONCEIVE the college of your dreams, BELIEVE it is in your grasp, and ACHIEVE what it takes to get there. Within view, within reach. Let's turn the light on and get going!

Bright Ideas

1. Look for the "bright ideas" highlighted throughout the book and the checklist of ideas at the end of each chapter.

2. Refer to these "bright ideas" to develop an action plan with your child to take the "next steps" on the college-bound journey.

2

Believing "Yes, I Can!"

"Don't worry** about the money yet."
When parents hear me say this, I
sense that many of them are ready
to strangle me on the spot because getting the
money for college can be such a stressful and time-
consuming challenge for families.

So let me just start by making one thing
clear: As you begin the college-bound journey,
it's important to believe you CAN do something
(such as afford college) instead of beginning with
"we can't afford College X." There will come a time
when counting the costs is necessary. But don't
let the fear of finances or anything else keep you
and your child from taking the right next steps to
explore options. Focus first on the objective, going
to college, and then later we will focus on the costs
of getting there.

Begin with the End in Mind

A friend of mine told me the story of her first day of orientation on a new college campus. The dean of the school led all the freshmen students out to the center of the campus and told them, "This is where you will be. This is where you will sit on graduation day. I will be standing up here, on stage, and you will walk across this stage where I will hand you your diploma." The dean was determined that these new students, most of whom were overwhelmed and scared with the huge tasks, endless classes, and four years ahead, would SEE and BELIEVE that their dream of graduating from college would become a reality.

In the first chapter, I shared with you the three important steps on the college-bound journey:

Conceive it.

Believe it.

Achieve it.

In the first chapter, we talked about the journey in order to see what lies ahead: to shed light, focus and bring the dream **WITHIN VIEW**. In this chapter, I want you to focus on BELIEVING that you and your child will successfully complete this journey and bring the dream **WITHIN REACH**.

Silence the Nay-Sayers

So, what are the common obstacles for you and your child believing, "Yes, I can?" In my own experience, and through the testimonies of others, I have heard folks say that once they declare they are headed to college, and especially to certain more selective colleges, they've been told, "You'll never get in there!" Too often, once you decide and publicly state your goal, you become the target of others who do not share your dreams or faith that you can achieve them. Some detractors, and even well-meaning advisors who try to help you "deal with reality," can unintentionally throw water on your child's dreams and create more obstacles for you and your child.

In my experience many parents are too quick to accept what the "nay-sayers" say. **Before you accept the opinions and advice of others that say "you can't," you need to ask your own questions. Visit college campuses and meet university administrators yourself. See with your own eyes, and hear with your own ears what is possible and a realistic expectation for your child. Get your facts about admissions criteria, financial aid and everything else from the source!**

Before you listen to the nay-sayers who say

"you can't" make sure to communicate clearly and consistently to your child: "Yes, you can go to college and I will help you get there." It's important for your child to know he has your support, even if you don't have all of the answers, or at this point, all the resources.

Parents and other adults who are committed to working with students are notorious for encouraging young people and telling them in some fashion, "You can do this" whether it's acing a math test, running a race, marching in the band, or making the team. Before Barack Obama could tell us as a nation, "Yes, we can" he had to first believe, "Yes, I can!" Obama had to be sure in himself that he was willing to do the work and to make the necessary sacrifices to become a successful young man, a star basketball player, the editor of the Harvard Law Review, a husband, father, United States Senator, and now President of the United States.

Identify the Obstacles

Without a doubt, parents never want to disappoint their children by raising hopes that are later dashed by others who tell them, for example: 1) Even though you can afford that college, you're not a good fit for that college, 2) "You can't afford that school," or 3) "The reason you will not make it past the first year of college is because your high school does not have a good reputation." These are real obstacles and challenges that you must address as we will do in this book. However, many parents and students give up too early and too easily on the possibility of college because of the worries and the work.

Granted, it is not enough to simply believe "Yes, I can." Your child must be willing to do the hard work and make the necessary sacrifices to achieve the goal of getting accepted to college. However, the first right step on the college-bound journey is to BELIEVE that you and your child CAN reach the college destination that is right for him.

Confidence, not arrogance, is essential for your child's college success. If you as a parent communicate with confidence to your child, "Yes, you can!," then he will begin to believe it as well.

One important step in believing "Yes, I can" is to make a list of concerns about the college application process and address them one by one. Make a list of all the things that concern you and your child the most about getting into and making good grades at your child's college of choice. This list may include having the money, finding the right school, living away from home, picking the right major, getting the necessary assistance for learning disabilities, or making new friends. For each item on the list, you and your child should brainstorm together ways to address the concern, obstacle or fear in making the dream of college a reality.

Sometimes, high school seniors can become almost paralyzed by the fear of not getting into college or not getting certain scholarships. Tears and temper tantrums are not uncommon as your teenager deals with the day to day grind of twelfth grade homework, SAT prep, clubs, sports, socializing, a part-time job, plus filling out all the necessary applications for college and financial aid.

I have had parents and students tell me that the amount of time and energy they spend on the college application process during the fall of the senior year is "exhausting and like having a part-time job."

Sometimes, I think parents and other adults become so focused on the end of the senior year and graduation that we forget that seventeen and eighteen year old high school seniors need time to adjust as they begin to realize "this is my very last year at my high school." Teenagers need time and space to adjust as they begin to ask the question: "What's next for me after high school?" Think about it. Every September since your child was five or six years old, he has probably known the school, the teacher and the classroom that would be his very own for that school year. With the start of your child's last year of high school, there are many unknowns about where your child will be living and what he will be doing the September after graduation from high school. This creates anxiety!

Remember the cartoon image from chapter one with the mouse that appeared as a huge monster? By shedding light on these fears – the "monster" – you realize that the fears and concerns are not as big or bad as they seemed.

Conceive it.

Believe it.

Achieve it.

To believe, "Yes, I can," you and your child must shed light on those fears and doubts, addressing, even silencing, the voices of the "nay-sayers," and instilling confidence in your child to do the hard work necessary. Mama used to say, "Where there is a will, there is a way." Once you and your child believe it, your child can achieve it if he does the hard work to make his dream a reality. The steps outlined in these chapters will help you and your child bring the dream of college admission *Within View and Within Reach*.

Bright Ideas

1.   Instead of focusing on the obstacles and the "No, you can't" of nay-sayers, ask your own questions to explore the possible options and "Yes, you can" for your child.

2.   Make a list of all the *worries, fears or concerns* that lead you and your child to doubt whether college admission is possible. Convert those worries, or concerns into *work* and an action plan that addresses those fears head on.

3

Tackling the Task as a Team

As with any journey, the college-bound journey is best NOT done alone! In fact, if you as a parent attempt this journey by yourself – especially without input from your child – you will likely regret it later. The college-bound process is a journey you make as a team. But who should you make sure is on this journey with you and your child?

Parents, It's Not about You!

Well, the most important person on the team is your child, the college-bound student! Parents, this exploration process is not about you and what you "woulda', coulda', shouda' done" when you were thirteen or seventeen. Nor is this journey about insuring that your child gets into the college you picked for him based on your own salary, title, friends, or the school from which you, your parents, or your grandparents graduated. Instead, this journey is about you and your teenager exploring as many options as possible to ensure that he enters the best college environment that will nurture, equip, and challenge him to become a successful, well-adjusted adult.

Let's face it. If most of us as adults had to do it over again, we might make different choices along the journey to adulthood. But the reality is, we cannot get those critical crossroad experiences back. However, we *can* share those experiences, both our mistakes and our successes, on the roads we have traveled to help guide teenagers as they face similar decisions.

Parents, you probably know what you want for your child, and you can honor this in the process. However, *your* wishes and dreams for your child should be considered in light of what *your child* wishes and dreams for himself.

Start Early

So, the first step is to engage your child in the

college exploration process. But how soon is too soon to talk about college with your child? It is never too early to speak positively about your own college experience and to instill in your children a desire to share those experiences. If you did not go to college, you might share your dream that your child go to college and introduce examples of family, friends, and others who did go to college. By middle school, students know more about colleges and start to form opinions including likes and dislikes, even if based only on college sports!

Any time you have the chance to take your child on a college campus – to the library, for a ball game or to simply walk around – do it! The more your child is exposed to college life, college opportunities, and discussions about jobs and careers, he will understand your expectations and aspirations for him.

As long as your teenager is thinking and talking about college in a positive manner, then you and your child are on your way to being college-bound.

But some of you may be wondering, "How do I even get him to talk about college?" Many parents complain that their children, especially their sons, stop sharing information about school and friends as they progress through the teenage years. This child who once talked your ears off from kindergarten through the sixth grade now has hair under his arms and mumbles when you ask him questions. Often during the teen years, many students stop sharing their "big dreams" and "big thoughts" with their parents for fear of being ridiculed by them or because it's not "cool" for teenagers to talk with their parents about these subjects!

During this time, teenagers are developing their own identities, trying out new sets of friends, driving on their own, and venturing into new territories where Mom and Dad are not always down the hall or a door away. While it may seem to parents that their teenagers are totally uninterested in conversations about college, career, and their futures in general, teens are often very eager to get your opinions on such matters. At times, they may not want you to know just how interested they are. Do not hold back on sharing your expectations, but don't overwhelm them either.

Listen to Their Dreams

Several years ago, I read about a fellow Morehead Scholar from Canada who said she always wanted to go to Mars from a very early age. She told her parents that she wanted to be a space traveler and even to land on Mars and live there. Over the years, I have followed this woman's career, and she became a Rhodes Scholar, as I did. Her travels have taken her all over the world as a leading researcher in her field. I have no doubt that if and when America, or China, or Bill Gates, or some other great entrepreneur sets up shop on Mars, this woman will be part of the pilot team who makes it happen. But what if, at the tender age of seven or eight, her parents had told her that she was foolish with all this talk about outer space and going to live on Mars? What if her parents had tried to talk her out of her dreams and instead talked her into becoming something much more reasonable, like an accountant or a doctor?

Parents, more than you realize, your children want you to be excited about what excites them. But **to know and support the dreams of your child, you must take time to listen to him!** Only then, once you listen and reflect on these dreams with him, can you rest assured that you will not miss out on being a part of it, or even worse, that he gives up on his dreams altogether.

Some parents express disappointment when their child has only one goal: to be a professional athlete. But if that's what excites him, see how serious he is by asking probing questions about that career as well as other careers and options that are available. If video games and ESPN are the only sources of information your child is using to explore college and careers, then his options will be limited. However, you have the golden opportunity to introduce new people, new TV programs and helpful resources to expand your child's range of options. If your child cannot see for himself the options available in this future, you can help him bring those opportunities *within his view and within his reach.*

If your child is not talking about his dreams or college at all, it could be that he has decided that college immediately after high school is not for him. Or it could be that your child needs to talk with someone other than you to explore college and other options, including part-time or full-time employment or enlisting in the military. Allow your child to voice his true desires, keeping all honorable options open except doing nothing.

Other Adults on the Team

If your child does not seem willing to talk with you, ask him if he is willing to talk with another adult and offer him that opportunity. Most children will talk about their hopes and dreams if someone who is genuinely interested is willing to listen. He may not be talking to you directly, but instead he may be talking to others including friends, relatives, teachers, or advisors.

In fact, the same child who may act like he does not hear you at all may suddenly morph into an intelligent, sane, and even mature young adult in the presence of aunts, uncles, ministers, teachers and coaches. But parents, do not take this personally. Your child's tendency to open up around others is less about you and more about him and his need to expand his world and circle of influence. Instead of being threatened by your child's openness to others, encourage these other dialogues and make opportunities to interject your own opinions at strategic times.

From sixth grade to twelfth grade, almost all the adults surrounding me (my parents, other relatives, ladies at church, teachers, and others in the community) communicated the same messages to me.

- Stay focused, keep up your grades.

- Everybody is not your friend.

- Do unto others as you would have them do unto you.

- Keep your legs closed!

Now, as uncomfortable as it may be, we adults need to be more intentional and more direct with teenagers about the influence of peer pressure, hormones, and the need to be liked and accepted, especially by the opposite sex. Not addressing these topics consistently from middle to high school and throughout college is to keep potential obstacles "in the dark" and risk the stumbling blocks they may cause for your child along the college-bound journey.

Involve Your Child's Friends

For most teenagers, their social groups and interactions are critically important and cannot and should not be ignored. So how can you be sensitive to these needs while keeping your child focused on the college path?

First, take time to talk about college in the presence of your child and his friends, including friends of the opposite sex. Make college choices and careers a normal topic of conversation. Ask your child's friends about their hopes, dreams, and college possibilities. And from time to time ask your child's friends, in his presence, what special qualities and potentials they see in your child. You may be surprised and so will your teenager. The objective is to create an environment where constructive criticism works to everyone's mutual benefit. In focus groups with high school students, especially seniors, it has been interesting to learn how many students say that a friend's parent was a key factor or influence in their decision to go to college or pursue a certain career.

Talk openly as a family about the importance of guarding and protecting your children's dreams, including protecting and nurturing their bodies, minds, hearts, and souls. Talk openly about those things that could impede your child's path to success. And talk about the importance of associating with and surrounding himself with people who want to be as successful and as faithful on the journey as he does.

Talk to the Teachers

In addition to his peers, others who can help as part of the team are your child's teachers and advisors. Think about it. Unless you are home schooling, these adults spend more waking hours each day with your child than you do! Your child's teachers may see abilities and special aptitudes in your child that you have not seen before. Furthermore, these adults see your child engage with others in the classroom setting and may have great input in helping your child and you find the best college fit.

Other adults who provide important insights and influence for your child include counselors, church youth group leaders, coaches, employers, music and art instructors. Again, these adults see your child in various settings and circumstances, performing at his best and even sometimes his worst. They know how your child responds to new pressures and how he excels with new tasks. They have coached him and provided academic advising. All of these individuals have the opportunity to counsel, coach, encourage and hold your child accountable in taking his right next steps on the college-bound journey.

Establish an open and ongoing dialogue with your child's teachers, advisors, youth counselors, coaches, and instructors. Make college choices a normal part of your conversation and interactions with them. The purpose of these conversations is threefold: 1) to hear where they think your child should go to college, 2) to help "see" and understand your child from different viewpoints and 3) to have other voices of encouragement and support for your child when he is away from you.

Ultimately, the decision of where to go to college and how to get there is up to your child, with you as one of his guides. However, getting there often takes a team of family and friends, teachers and instructors, coaches and counselors. As a parent, you help guide this journey by assuring that others along that path are providing consistent, encouraging, and challenging messages that help your child make the right choice for him.

Without a doubt, the "core" of the team is found at home. Even though neither of my parents attended college, they had a clear sense of how this "team" should work when it came to my brothers and me. Throughout the course of my high school days, my mother was constantly telling us that our "job" was to keep our grades up and work hard in school. And even though we were to leave the money issues to Mom and Dad, they wanted us to understand the financial realities of the household. My brother, Bill, and I had jobs during the school year and summer. We used the money for clothes, entertainment and gas for the 1964 Malibu my father gave me in 1979.

My parents made it very clear that even though they worked hard and were saving for our education, they would not be able to pay the bill for sending all three of us to college. So, my brothers and I knew that our "job" was to make good grades and to do all we could to obtain scholarships. The rest of the family, our church and the community would keep us on track and discipline us when needed... all as a part of the team. We believed that if we all did our "job," then together we would get into college, get a degree and pursue the career of our dreams.

Mine was not the perfect household. But what I learned and now believe is that when parents are able to stick it out despite the difficulties, and when students hang in there and do the hard work despite distractions, together you will make it – as a team.

The Role of Parent on the Team

As a parent, you have a critically important role in nurturing the best of who your child is and the best he can accomplish. Two of my favorite movies that provide excellent examples about the role of parents in their child's academic aspirations are *Akeela and the Bee* and *The Ron Clark Story.* In *Akeela and the Bee,* Akeela and her mother are informed by her principal that she will be coached by a very important man for the spelling bee. When they learn that this extremely smart and successful man lives in their own South Central Los Angeles neighborhood, they are shocked. However, this neighborhood gentleman becomes an incredible resource to strengthen the best in Akeela. So our first lesson from *Akeela* is that in neighborhoods all around us, there are people who have phenomenal experiences and a wealth of knowledge who are willing to share if they are asked. Your next door neighbor, your neighbor in the pew, or your neighbor in the cubicle or corner office down the hall just might have the answer or advice you or your child needs to navigate this college-bound journey.

In *Akeela and the Bee*, we also see that Akeela's mother is very demanding. It is not until later in the movie we discover that her mother's singular goal is to protect Akeela from the hardships she had to endure. We also learn, as Akeela's mother did, that the best way to nurture and protect your child is to share your experiences and wisdom with him so he can soar higher than you or he ever dreamed.

In *The Ron Clark Story*, the daughter, who is one of Mr. Clark's best students, must come home immediately from school every day to provide child care and prepare dinner for her younger siblings. As a result, she is not able to dedicate the time and attention needed for her studies. So, her teacher, Mr. Clark, attempts to tell her mother how bright the daughter is. When he tries to convince her mother that the daughter is college material, his encouragement falls on deaf ears. But when Mr. Clark convinces the mother that the daughter is smart enough to attend the magnet school "across town," the mother finally realizes that she must relieve her daughter of other responsibilities so she can succeed at being a strong student. This student's mother, like Akeela's mother, had only known hardship. Once other possibilities are brought to light, the mother realizes that what seemed impossible to her is actually possible for her child.

Parents are often scared that their own limited experiences will limit the possibilities for their children. However, as we see with both these mothers, **letting go of your own fears and failures frees your children to achieve the dreams you never thought possible – for yourself or for them.**

The college-bound journey should never be taken alone – as a parent or as a student. To safely and effectively reach the desired destination, it requires a team where each member does his own part. **As you begin the college exploration process, set aside time as parent and child to talk about this journey together including the responsibilities you each have to make it smooth and successful.** As you see the need along the way, involve others in the discussion, and therefore the journey, too. Getting accepted at the college of your child's dreams and maintaining a balanced academic and social life are no small tasks. To tackle this task, it takes a team to bring options and realistic goals *Within View* and *Within Reach.*

Bright Ideas

1. Take your children of all ages on college campuses every chance you get.

2. Listen to and reflect on the dreams and aspirations of your child as often as you can. Make note of these emerging dreams, even if they tell you they want to live on Mars or play in the NBA.

3. Offer your child the opportunity to talk to other trusted adults about his life dreams.

4. Include your child's friends in open conversations about college and career plans.

5. Protect and nurture your child's body, mind, and soul.

6. Establish an open and ongoing dialogue about your child's future plans and choices with school counselors, college advisors, teachers, coaches and others on your team.

7. Openly nurture discussion among the "core" of your team, your family, and talk about each family member's responsibilities on the college-bound journey.

8. Let go of your own fears and failures of the past and uncertainty about the future to free your child to achieve success.

4

Making the Grade

No **parent** wants to wipe away the tears of a dejected high school senior who does not get into his number one choice for college. But these days, it's important to approach the college-bound journey understanding that the competition for entering two and four year colleges is greater than ever. And grades DO matter!

Parents, when many of you came through high school, the focus was solely on the grades you received and grade point average. I often hear parents talk about how their children are making straight A's so they should be guaranteed admission into the college of their choice and should have plenty of scholarship money. However, making straight A's, being in the top ten and even scoring close to perfect on standardized tests are no longer guarantees for college admissions, much less full scholarships.

Build on Academic Strengths

As Americans, we are great at identifying and developing athletic potential and talent, but we sometimes struggle to identify and develop academic potential and talent. When a young person in our community, especially a boy, exhibits athletic prowess, we buy him the best equipment, make sure he is well fed, and give him plenty of rest! From a young age, we make sure he has the right coaches and the opportunities to compete at the highest level possible to improve himself and gauge himself with the best in the talent pool. As a community, we all pitch in to ensure that he has everything he needs to chart his path toward an athletic scholarship to the college of his choice.

But what happens when a student demonstrates equal strength in academics? Imagine if we prepared our students with academic prowess to be our most competitive math students, French students, or drafting students. What if we sent college recruiters and corporate headhunters in the poorest neighborhoods, the most rural, and the lowest-performing high schools and local libraries looking for the outstanding academic talent? Nike, Adidas, the National Football League, National Basketball Association, Major League Baseball and Major League Soccer send out their scouts to turn every rock, climb every stair, and go to the far corners of our neighborhoods to find the best athletic talent in the world. But we must do an equal, if not better, job creating the academic pipeline to connect our extraordinary students – regardless of race, income or zip code – with the extreme wealth and resources found in our nation's colleges and universities.

As parents, *you cannot wait* for the recruiters and headhunters to come find your child. Instead, **you need to find ways to connect your child's academic ability and interests with the college settings where he will thrive and where the college will benefit from his presence and participation.**

Increase Rigor

Nowadays, the focus is not only on grades but on rigor. When presented with the "My child makes straight A's" introduction from parents, I ask: "What level were your child's courses? College preparatory (CP)? Honors? Advanced Placement (AP)? International Baccalaureate (IB)?" In many instances, the parents cannot tell me because their focus is solely on the grade, not the rigor or challenge the course represents and how it fits in to the student's overall transcript. Often, parents get comfortable with their children's success as a high achiever at the middle school level. But at some point, parents must work directly with the school to find ways in which their child can compete and thrive academically by knowing that he is taking the most challenging and rigorous courses offered. To prepare your child for the college-bound journey, you must **learn how to construct a course load, course sequencing, and transcript that most adequately prepares him as a competitive applicant to the college which matches his needs.**

In talking with your child's school, you might ask: 1) Is my child on grade level in reading and math? 2) Is my child taking the right courses to be eligible for admission to a four-year college? If you do not understand how to read or interpret your child's report card, transcript, progress reports or standardized test results (PSAT, SAT, ACT, AP), then *get some help.* You should never assume your child is doing "just fine" if you don't get a call from the school or e-mail from a teacher.

While it was once thought that Advanced Placement (AP) classes could level the playing field for many of America's high school students, research now shows that the quality and effectiveness of the AP teacher may be a better indicator of success on the AP exams. After completing the challenge and requirements of the AP course, some students refuse to take the exam since they do not believe their teacher prepared them sufficiently to score the necessary points to secure college credits for the course. So if students are not taking the final AP exam, why take the course? The answer: so they will be better prepared to perform in college-level classes and to get the "weighted" or "quality" points that will improve their overall grade point average.

During the 2008 elections, I watched an interview with Michelle Obama. She talked about taking AP courses during the 1970s at her high school in Chicago which helped prepare her for Princeton University. I remember sitting there thinking, "Wait a minute. I'm the same age as Michelle, but I never knew AP courses were taught back then!" It was not until the late 1980s that AP courses made it to my hometown high school, and the International Baccalaureate (IB) program has not arrived yet! Too often I hear parents say, "Well, I'm still waiting to see what our school will offer." But when it comes to your child, you are his greatest advocate, and as a tax payer or as one who pays tuition, you have the voice to say what your child needs.

The more competitive it is to be accepted to a college, the higher the expectations will be that your child has taken the most rigorous academic courses available at his school and that his grade point average reflects progress toward that goal. For some students, however, the ninth grade year or their experience with a particular subject proved to be such a challenge that the courses taken by the student were not the most rigorous the school offered but they were the most rigorous for that particular student. In other words, your child should demonstrate that he has given his best effort both in course selection and grades. By the twelfth grade, the academic transcript is your child's "academic resume." The transcript tells a story of your child's high school academic career and is a critical element in the college application process.

Map It Out

So as a parent, how do you best ensure that your child is doing what he can to enter into and succeed at the college of his dreams? First, do not wait until his junior or senior year to consider course sequence or rigor. **As early as seventh and eighth grade begin mapping out with your child and his school the courses he wants and needs to best prepare him to compete academically.** In coordination with your child and his school, you can determine which areas of study will require more work to make him competitive for certain colleges and scholarships. Look at what academic courses your child's school offers. Gain an understanding of which courses, course pathways or sequences are the least challenging and most challenging. Many colleges are not expecting your child to take every AP or IB course. But they will look to see if he has demonstrated the willingness and ability to take and succeed in the most challenging courses for him.

In some respects, you may not have control of specific classes or times that classes are offered at your child's school. For example, some classes are not taught every semester or every year. Student demand for classes or even availability of teachers can dictate if, when and what time of the day courses are offered. If your child wants to take courses with a certain teacher or courses for college credit (online, at his school, or on a college campus), you must plan ahead to do that while making sure that all other high school graduation requirements are met.

At several points during your child's middle school and high school career, at least twice a year, **make an appointment with your child's school counselor or college advisor who can help you**

and your child to establish the "right" course selection and sequencing to create the most challenging and appropriate academic experience for your child.

Often, students and parents do not pay attention to course selection and sequencing until much later in the student's academic career when graduation is a year or so away. The process of building a strong transcript can start as early as elementary school or middle school. For instance, a student who is stronger in math in elementary and early middle school will be ready to take algebra by the eighth grade. This course sequencing allows the student to take upper level math courses in high school that will strengthen his transcript and better prepare him for college level math.

If you cannot get an appointment with the school counselor or college adviser or if you want another opinion about courses your child should take, meet with the principal or a teacher who has been at the school for several years and is experienced in helping students navigate course selection. If you cannot get an appointment with the principal or an experienced teacher, **find a parent whose child graduated from your high school recently and has successfully made the transition into college.** Ask the family if they are willing to share their child's transcript, or at least to tell you the courses the student completed at your high school to get where they are. Attend open houses, teacher conferences, and volunteer at the school to meet other parents and share information about courses and school offerings. If all else fails, **find a teacher, coach, or another trusted individual to help you get the answers you need to support your child's academic journey.** The sooner you do this, the better you will understand what is expected of your child in high school and ultimately, in college.

Get Involved Early and Often

On far too many occasions, I meet parents who do not become intimately involved in their child's academic experience until the senior year of high school. And far too often, these parents or grandparents had expected that the school counselor, college advisor, a teacher, or the student himself was monitoring his status in meeting high school graduation requirements and college admissions criteria to make their child a competitive college applicant. In reality, many teenagers will select easier academic courses, do the least amount of work possible, and fail to tell you when critical events are happening at their school that could keep you informed. But parents, you must remember: YOU ARE THE PARENT! **Whether your child is at the top or the bottom of his class, every student needs an adult advocate to check on his grades, behavior, peer groups, and any other matters that promote or distract from his emotional and physical health and motivation to graduate successfully.** And that advocate, parent, must be YOU! Being a custodial parent, or legal guardian, is the only qualification you need to walk into your child's school and check on how your child is doing. Every school and every student must have a system of checks and balances to monitor progress. Your child and the school need to know that you are keeping up with what is going on at all times.

Other Opinions

No matter how involved you are as a parent, the other reality is that you cannot be all places at all times. As a parent, you are not always objective about your child! Therefore, **you also need other trusted and more objective eyes and ears to offer honest and constructive feedback on your child.** A family friend, or colleague, who will tell you the truth, no matter what, is priceless. For instance, ask a family friend to interview your child and offer constructive criticism to improve his skills and comfort when interviewing with others. Granted, your child may be embarrassed by doing so, but it is better to experience the discomfort of a poor mock interview with a trusted family member or friend than to blow a scholarship interview because your child is not prepared.

My mother worked in the school system, and many people in town would call her or stop by our house to ask my mother's interpretation about how their child was doing in school. Sometimes they would bring a report card or a teacher's note about their child to get my mother's opinion about what was really being said. Likewise, when my parents learned that I was identified as "Academically and Intellectually Gifted" (AIG) by our school system, my mother sought out teachers and parents who could help her understand what she needed to do to keep me challenged and progressing.

Standardized Tests

Make sure your child is prepared for and takes standardized tests such as the PSAT, SAT or ACT. Because grades can sometimes be subjective, standardized tests help college admission officers compare your child's performance in his school with students across the nation in a broader fashion. These test scores are used by some summer camps and after school programs, such as Duke TIP, to gauge your child's potential and promise as early as middle school. The general thought is that your child's academic performance,   grades, and class rank combined with SAT or ACT scores will better predict how well he will perform at the college level. SAT Reasoning Test (SAT, formerly known as the Scholastic Aptitude Test) assesses your child's knowledge in three primary areas: critical reading skills, mathematical skills, and writing skills. The ACT (American College Testing) assesses basic skills in five areas: English, math, reading, science reasoning, and writing. Check with the colleges your child is interested in and see what, if any, standardized tests they require.

Studies have shown that preparing for and taking sample tests do improve student test scores. So encourage your child to do it! Many students can also improve their test scores by taking the actual test more than once, so allow time and money for two to three "takes" if possible. Also, do not forget the PSAT (Preliminary Scholastic Achievement Test) which can be taken as early as middle school so your child can become more comfortable and familiar with standardized tests and test-taking skills.. The PSAT also helps to determine those areas where your child needs to focus and be better prepared for taking the SAT and/or ACT.

Among other things, college admission officers

look at class rank and the student's overall transcript as key indicators of your child's performance in high school. The essays, letters of recommendation, and extracurricular activities along with the transcript paint a picture of the kind of person and student your child really is. Just remember, no one indicator is sufficient to give the full picture of your child's past performance or potential. Though they can be helpful, letters of recommendation are sometimes regarded as too subjective. Grade point averages can also be confusing since some are weighted, others are not. And standardized test scores such as the SAT or ACT are not even required by some major universities as part of their application process. For example, Wake Forest University no longer requires the SAT, yet its freshmen classes are as academically competitive and more diverse than ever. And yet the importance of standardized tests cannot be overlooked. Therefore, all these elements together more fully tell your child's story of how he can become a successful and desirable college student.

More Than a Grade

Time and time again, I hear representatives from colleges and universities emphasize that grades are important, but they do not provide the full picture of what they are looking for in incoming students.

A few years ago, I attended an information session with admission representatives from Harvard, Duke, and the University of Pennsylvania. Each representative said, in his or her own way, "If we wanted a freshman class of all students who made perfect scores on the SAT or had straight A's all through high school, we could do that. But it is not just about the scores. Yes, academic performance indicators are important, but we are really looking for students who have *passion* about something and pursue it. We are looking for students who are making contributions to their community and will make a contribution to ours."

Additionally, help your child identify that passion through which he is able to make a difference in the world around him no matter how small that "world" may be! Watch for the spark or what excites him, whether it's sports, the arts, the sciences, or volunteering. Encourage your child to put those passions into action by engaging in the community in ways that he knows he can, and does, make a difference and is able to articulate that to others.

Grade Thirteen

The reality may be that you and your high school senior may decide that he is not yet academically ready to begin college immediately after graduating from high school.

In response to this growing need, **some schools offer what is known as "Grade 13" or post-graduate high school studies to better prepare students for the transition to college.** One example of such a school is Hargrave Military Academy. According to Hargrave's self-description as stated on their web site: www.hargrave.edu:

"Hargrave Post-Graduate cadets focus on critical English and math SAT/ACT skills in their first post-high school year. Classes are carefully selected to develop core skills and to challenge students in preparation for their freshman year in college. Students work within NCAA guidelines to improve their Core Course GPA in addition to working to improve their SAT/ACT scores. Success in their post graduate courses also strengthens their high school transcript as they apply to colleges of their choice."

Getting the Edge

Making the grade means being prepared academically and emotionally for college, and this preparation needs to begin early. The following are some specific ways that your child can develop a more competitive edge.

If there is one thing I would scream from the mountaintop to parents, it would be this: "Send your child to a summer camp!" Academic, athletic, leadership, and music summer camps, among others, allow your child, and you, to prepare for the college-bound journey by exposing him to a college campus, interfacing with other challenging students, and allowing him to survive, and even thrive, away from home.

First, summer camps allow your child to be on his own without your direct supervision. If they can admit it, many parents struggle as much as their children during periods of prolonged separation such as a one week, one month or summer-long overnight camp. However, the experience of your child being away for weeks (or over a month) will be good practice for both of you for that first year of college. If neither of you are ready for an overnight camp, you might consider day camps as you both prepare for longer stays.

Summer camp is also a great opportunity to teach your child to be responsible for his needs day to day. Some children struggle to keep up with their belongings when they live under your roof. But when they have to live with peers for a week or so, they get the hang of being more responsible if for no other reason than to avoid embarrassment by peers or camp counselors. Granted, summer camp is not the total remedy for helping teens become more responsible. However, the experience does help establish a healthy independence that will be good for both you and your child.

Going to summer camps, especially ones that will expose him to other students across the state, the country, or the world, will also teach your child that there are lots of other smart and talented kids! You may repeatedly tell your child, "There are other kids who are smarter, bigger, faster, or more talented than you." But until he experiences it personally, he may continue to be the "legend in his own mind." When students get an "up close and personal" look at the competition academically, artistically and athletically, their motivation to work hard often increases. Additionally, these opportunities allow your child to interface with students from many different regions, beliefs, and experiences so he can begin to expand his world and horizons.

Beginning as early as the fourth grade and extending through high school, I attended Girl Scout, leadership, and sports camps that shaped both how I engaged my world and others and sharpened who I was and how I performed. These experiences taught me team work, hard work, how to win with passion and how to lose with grace.

All of these experiences stretched me academically, athletically, and culturally. One of the most formative summer experiences for me was North Carolina Governor's School the summer between my sophomore and junior years of high school. It was there that I encountered for the first time hundreds of passionate, competitive students from across North Carolina who were as smart – if not smarter –than me! And it was the first time I was surrounded by a large and socioeconomically diverse group of other Black students who were all ambitious, well-rounded, opinionated, and college-bound. After that summer, I returned to my high school determined to work harder because I had seen what was possible, and I had been challenged to achieve it. Getting an "up close and personal" residential summer camp experience less than an hour from home alongside several hundred of North Carolina's top students showed me my strengths, weaknesses and exactly what things I needed to work on during the last two years of high school.

Remember in school when we used to ask, "Will this homework assignment or test count toward our grade?" When it comes to your child presenting himself to the college of his choice, everything counts! So, to make the grade, start early, be intentional, and look at the big picture. Of all the aspects of the college-bound journey, this is one you must consider earlier versus later. Making the grade requires slow, steady, and intentional progress toward the goals to bring college admission *Within View* and *Within Reach*. So start now!

Chapter Four Bright Ideas

1. Begin focusing on your child's academic abilities, strengths, and interests so together you can match those with the best college environment for him.

2. Construct a rigorous academic course load for your child that will challenge him but not overwhelm him.

3. Make sure your child takes rigorous academic courses if he plans on applying to a "selective" college.

4. Map out with your child's school your child's sequence of courses (beginning as early as the sixth or seventh grade) to achieve his academic goals.

5. Make an appointment to meet at least twice a year with your child's school counselor or college advisor.

6. Consult with a trusted and experienced teacher,

another "seasoned" adult to answer your questions about your child's academic journey.

7. Be your child's active advocate to make sure he is getting what he needs.

8. Check in on your child with other trusted adults who will give you constructive, honest feedback.

9. Make sure your child is prepared for and takes standardized tests (PSAT, SAT, ACT) at least twice to improve scores.

10. Focus on strengthening your child's passion and interest to identify the unique contribution he will make to a college community.

11. Consider Grade 13 post-graduate high school studies to better prepare for the college transition.

12. Help your child "get an edge" and stronger experience and exposure through summer academic, athletic, or leadership camps on college campuses.

5

Finding the Right Fit

One of the most important steps in determining which college is best for your child is to think clearly about what kind of college environment will provide the best fit. I often tell parents and students that there are more than 3,000 colleges and universities in the United States. And even within these choices, there are a variety of options including online, community college, two and four year colleges and universities. When considering where your child should go to college, remember: It's not where you start, but rather where and with what degree and experiences you finish. There truly is a college to meet your child's needs. So, the question is not IF there is a college out there for him, but rather which college will provide the best fit.

Ask the Right Questions and Lots of Them!

When assessing the "right fit" for your child, you need to consider several aspects that have shaped the student and person your child is today:

- His past and current learning environments and how they have impacted him.
- His current school's academic offerings and performance.
- His level of engagement and challenge,
- His academic performance.
- His comfort with and need for social engagement with others.
- His ability to be a self-starter.
- Your comfort level to "let go."

First, let's take a look at your child's learning environment by asking the questions found in Appendix 5-A.

Once you have a handle on the environment where your child will be most comfortable to grow and learn, then you should assess the learning environment where your child is now. **To compare your child's school's performance with others in the nation, answer the questions in Appendix 5-B.**

Your local school system, state departments of

education, the College Board (www.collegeboard. com) and ACT (www.act.org) web sites are a few sources that provide information about your child's school or school system as compared to other schools and school systems across your state and the nation. By looking at these comparisons, you can better understand how college admissions officers are comparing your child with other applicants from the same school and from different schools nationwide. Students at lower-performing schools often do not believe that they can compete academically with students from other school systems within their own state or across the nation. The reality is that the transition from high school to college is a challenge for most students. However, if your child understands his own strengths and weaknesses compared to that of other students, he can better prepare himself to be a more competitive applicant.

While parents want and expect their children to do their best, HOW your child exerts himself will also determine what kind of college will best suit him. **To determine the level of challenge your child typically engages in and his level of performance, ask yourself and your child the questions found in Appendix 5-C.** These questions help assess where your child has excelled as well as struggled and how he performs compared to others.

Five | Finding the Right Fit

Students and parents often do not take enough time to review and analyze feedback from standardized tests. For example, a serious review of your child's PSAT, SAT, or ACT report should help you understand your child's strengths and weaknesses, and in turn, what he needs to work on to improve his score a second, third, or fourth time around. Additionally, testing companies provide names of students to colleges and universities, and as a result, students receive mail from colleges they have never heard of. Often students never open these mailings, much less share this information with you. However, these mailings come as a result of some "match" or "fit" based on survey information or personal data your child provided or from referrals made by teachers, coaches, counselors, or alumni.

Parents, you may wish to avoid meddling in the affairs of your eleventh or twelfth grader. But in reality, many twelfth graders do not know the questions they need to ask to explore their options. Unless you, as the parent, ask to see these letters, brochures, scholarship applications, and other offers your child receives, your child may not know that he has a gold mine in his hands! These communications from colleges may contain invitations to Open Houses in your city or state or applications for specific scholarships. If overlooked, your child may miss that "jewel" which may meet his needs and provide scholarship money simply because he did not open his mail or reply to e-mail.

Life Beyond the Classroom

As we know, college is more than academics. The college experience can greatly shape and transform who your child will become and how he engages the world around him as an adult. Therefore, it is also important to assess how he currently engages others socially to determine the right fit for the college years. **To find the best college environment to nurture your child socially, ask yourself and your child the questions found in Appendix 5-D.**

Beyond the classroom, there is a lot to consider about your child and the new school environment that will best suit him. For some students, the opportunity to participate in sporting events, or at least attend them, is critically important. While many students participated in high school sports, the opportunity and desire to do so at the collegiate level will vary from school to school and student to student. The same is true with other extracurricular activities such as marching band, chorus, debate team, or drama. Furthermore, the decision whether or not to participate in college athletics and other extracurricular activities is more than a matter of making the team, or scholarships that may be available. At the college level, these activities place significant demands on a student's time and can vary greatly depending on the activity, the coach, and the level of competition.

During my freshman year at the University of North Carolina, I was very eager to join clubs because that was what I had always done when I was in high school and middle school. However, my decision to play varsity basketball dictated everything else about my day and my school year. I thought I might like to play in the band, but that was out of the question because the demands of the band would directly conflict with the demands of basketball, not to mention adapting to the college freshman workload and reading requirements. After consulting with my suite mate, who was a committee chair at the Student Union, she encouraged me to serve on the "University Day" Committee which was responsible for the school's birthday celebration. Serving birthday cake on University Day to hundreds of people was the extent of my other extracurricular activities my freshman year. Every other minute was committed to class, studying, basketball, and surviving the transition from home-life to college life.

Readiness to Let Go

All of these questions will help you and your child discern his readiness for the college experience, but what about you? **You and your child need to have honest and open discussions regarding the readiness to "let go."** The discussion should encompass both your readiness and his readiness to let go. The following questions will also help you take an honest look at your own level of readiness and how this may impact the "best fit" for your child: How prepared are you to let your child make mistakes and to allow him to learn from these mistakes without your help? How far away from home are you prepared to let your child go to college? Thirty minutes? Two hours? Six hours? A plane ride? If your child has a roommate of a different race or religion, how will you respond? If your child begins dating someone of a different race or religion, how will you respond? If travel abroad is a college option or a requirement, are you prepared to let your child participate?

For many students, and for some of you as parents, your child's college experience may be the first exposure to people from different cultures, races, religions, regions, or nations. Even though I considered myself fairly well-travelled as a high school and college student, until my time as a graduate student at Oxford University in England, I did not realize just how much of a "North Carolina" or "American" experience I had lived. Until Oxford, I simply did not have the exposure to students of very diverse cultures and from many parts of the world. It is not that UNC did not offer that diversity. I had not actively sought it. At state universities, such as UNC, in-state students can be 80% or more of the student body. Students at many private universities come from across the US and around the world, so the opportunity to room with, study with, travel with and socialize with students at a place like Oxford was truly eye-opening.

Your child's desire for and comfort level with diversity and distance from home will play a big part in determining if an in-state or out-of-state school will be the best fit for your child. Several of the questions suggested above refer to your child's comfort and experience in being away from home. Prior to college some students have spent significant time away from home with great ease. Others have not even wanted to spend a night away. As you and your child consider different college choices, the question of living at home versus living away, including significant distance, is a crucial one.

For some students, it is an important act of independence to select an out-of-state school. For others, they are willing to overcome the fear of being farther away from home to attend the school that meets other essential "right fit" criteria. And for others, the need to be closer to home is critically important to provide the comfort needed to focus their energies on studies.

To avoid or at least minimize the impact of homesickness during your child's freshman year, **consider having your child attend an overnight summer camp during middle school and especially prior to his junior year of high school.** These types of extended away-from-home stays allow your child to experience, in part, what it will be like to be away from home and to live with someone else. Additionally, these experiences give you insight into what issues might need to be addressed when considering distance for you and your child in the college choice.

Another option not often considered is sending your child to summer school or some type of "Bridge" program at the college or university shortly after his high school graduation. Many students and parents view the summer between finishing high school and starting college as an opportunity to relax and do nothing. Conversely, some students and parents have used the summer to gain college credit, meet new college friends, get settled into dorm life and learn the campus while only a fraction of students and faculty are in town before the fall semester starts.

What to Ask the College?

Up to this point, as we have considered the "right fit," we have focused primarily on your child and what has shaped him to this point. However, in determining the "right fit," you also need to look at several aspects of the different schools. **Look at Appendix 5-E to find some key questions to ask of the colleges you are exploring.**

Even in middle school, when students talk about the specific colleges they are interested in, I strongly encourage them to go to that college's web site and find information about the types of students that attend that institution. The types of information elementary, middle and high school students can find on the college web sites include: What are the primary fields of study (majors) offered? How many AP courses did most incoming freshmen take in high school? How many hours of volunteering did incoming freshmen participate in each month in high school? How many students applied? How many or what percentage of students were accepted? Enrolled?

This information and more is often found under a "Freshman Profile" link on the college's web site.

Within View, Within Reach

This document gives an overview of the entering or enrolled freshman class. On this site, you may find average GPA, median SAT or ACT scores, the percentage of students in the top ten percent of their classes, as well as the states and regions from which the students come or even how much financial aid the freshman class received. You can use this information to help you understand how your child compares or will fit in with other students who are currently enrolled.

Alumni from colleges in which your child is interested can also be very helpful to give insights and tips about their alma mater. Of course, alumni should never make any promises to your child about getting accepted, but they may be able to offer specific information or contacts that can help your child navigate the application process. Also, make sure to ask local alumni about scholarships that are offered through the local or regional alumni chapters that may be available to your child.

Matching Interests and Offerings

In assessing the proper fit for your child, your child's interests are a major factor. At some point, you and your child need to discuss his anticipated field of study or proposed college major. Some college bound students have pre-determined their major before ever stepping on a college campus, or so they think! Other students take the first two years of college or more to determine their major. Either way, it's important to at least discuss your child's interests and explore those schools that are strongest in these subject areas. The reality is some schools are significantly better or stronger in certain majors by virtue of their tradition, founding purpose, faculty, location, or resources. Additionally, **look for schools that provide adequate supervision and academic advising along the way especially in those first two years of college to guide your child in that important discernment process.** Course sequencing at the college level is critical just like it was at the high school level.

As mentioned above, some students are not only clear on their major, they also think they have a clear picture of the career path they want to follow. If your child seems to have this path more clearly marked, **you may also want to factor in graduate school connections and options in your discussions as you determine the right undergraduate fit.** If your child is considering a career as a doctor, lawyer, professor, accountant or any number of professions which require additional schooling beyond a bachelor's degree, you may want to consider this when looking for the right undergraduate fit. If your child considers this now, he will be better prepared to find the right fit for graduate school, too.

As I was planning and ultimately deciding where I would go to college, I also believed that I wanted to go to law school. So when I was considering colleges, I was also mindful of how graduates from these colleges fared when applying to law schools. But, of course, I did not realize at the time how important my undergraduate experience would be in preparing me for the graduate school experience and more importantly for the world of work I would face throughout adulthood.

Often parents and students alike have asked me: "What were the key factors in your decision to attend the University of North Carolina instead of Harvard or Duke?" During my senior year in high school, 1980-1981, there was no such thing as the internet, so I had to rely on brochures, word of mouth and college tours. The more I thumbed through all the brochures and information from Harvard, Duke and North Carolina, one resource in particular stood out for me: the *Directory of Morehead Scholar Alumni from the University of North Carolina*. The more I flipped through the pages of that book, the more I read about Morehead Scholarship recipients from North Carolina, the United States, and even around the world who came to UNC for college. But most importantly, I saw their occupations after graduation from UNC, the graduate schools they attended, and the other opportunities that were open to them. Morehead scholars went on to law school at Harvard. They went on to Wall Street and around the world. As I read the biographies of the graduates in the Morehead Directory and the paths these alumni had taken to follow their dreams, I realized that I, too, wanted to follow that path, take advantage of the unique summer internships and access to an incredible alumni network!

Your child has options that will open up different paths to his dreams. As a parent, guardian or advocate, the key is helping him light the path to see, understand and evaluate what that future looks like and which college choice will best open the path before him and prepare him for the journey.

Public vs. Private

Another common question in finding the right fit is whether a public/state univeristy or private university is best. For most students and parents, the only real distinction between the two is the price tag! However, this should not be the first or only determining factor you examine when considering the right college for your child.

Financial Aid packages at some private universities are much more generous now. So make sure you are comparing "apples-to-apples" in your analysis of financial aid. For some families, you may want or need a particular religious or philosophical environment that is found at many private institutions. In turn, you may also be looking for a university, whether public or private, that may offer research opportunities for undergraduate students through their teaching hospitals or centers for academic excellence. **Both public and private colleges and universities offer "the best" of what your child may need, but be cautious and aware of what is really being offered and at what cost.**

These are only the beginning of many questions I have heard and continue to hear from parents over the last 25 years. To find the answers, you will need to spend time talking with your child, your child's teachers and school administrators, as well as forming critical questions to ask of the colleges you will be exploring. Additionally, I have found that **one of the best sources of information for you as parents are other parents of college students and recent college graduates.** Talk to them, and listen carefully and openly. They often provide a wealth of knowledge and helpful wisdom as ones who have recently walked this college-bound journey ahead of you!

Ask an Alumnus

A college's alumni association web page and its local chapter members also provide important glimpses into the school. In addition to the insights they provide, your child's initiative to interface with alumni could also payoff! For example, a few years ago I worked with two students who were interested in attending North Carolina State University (NCSU). As eleventh graders, they both voiced interest in becoming engineers, so I directed them to the web page about summer camps on NCSU's campus. The cost of these kinds of summer camps can range from free to thousands of dollars. During that same week, NCSU had recruiters in the area sponsoring a luncheon for prospective students at a local restaurant. One of these students attended the luncheon to personally express his interest in the school and to learn more about the engineering program and summer camp opportunities. At the end of the luncheon, he told the recruiter his interest in attending the summer camp, and the recruiter awarded him a scholarship to attend on the spot!

Because of this student's personal initiative to look up information on the school, attend the local event, and express his interest directly to a university representative, he was rewarded. A year later, he was accepted at NCSU but decided to attend Campbell University, a small, private institution, because of an opportunity to play football. However, the fact remains that his initiative paid off well for him and made him a role model for other students in his community.

One Size Does Not Fit All!

At the same time you are trying to determine if a school is the best fit for your child, remember that each school is also examining your child to decide if he is the best fit for them. As college admissions officers begin inquiring about your child, they, too, are examining your child's school and your child. With more than 3000 institutions of higher education across the country, each of these colleges has different admission requirements. One size does not fit all! From the most selective colleges to those with open admissions where anyone can attend, each institution has developed profiles of students they want to attract and those who have become successful graduates of their institution.

At most colleges, the Admission Offices have extraordinary amounts of information about individual high schools and how they compare with other high schools in their communities, state, and region. Information these Admission

Offices review include the courses the school offers (including number and type of AP and IB courses), the strength of the faculty, the courses offered to their students from local community or four-year colleges, graduation rates and drop-out rates of students as well as the number of students who have been admitted from a particular high school and the students degree completion rate. In addition to this information, Admission Offices also contract with other organizations, such as The College Board, which specialize in helping the college understand their "potential customers." For this reason, The College Board has a variety of fee-based services offered to both families and universities to help them "locate" each other.

Considering "Other" Options

Over the past ten to fifteen years especially, community colleges have become a more viable choice for many students to get a two year degree or certification before going into the workforce or then transferring to a college to complete their bachelor's degree. Community colleges are becoming an even more important player in the higher education landscape of America as four year colleges grow increasingly more expensive and competitive.

Some students need additional life experience to prepare them for college. One mother knew without a doubt that her son was not ready for college since she and her husband struggled to motivate him to finish high school. Other students want or need time off between high school and college, and they are looking for additional volunteer or travel experiences. For these individuals, AmeriCorps, as one example, may address their needs. AmeriCorps describes the program as follows:

"AmeriCorps is an opportunity to make a big difference in your life and in the lives of others around you. It's a chance to apply your skills and ideals toward helping others and meeting critical needs in the community. Each year, AmeriCorps offers 75,000 opportunities for adults of all ages and backgrounds to serve through a network of partnerships with local and national nonprofit groups." (http://www.americorps.gov/)

In addition to the experience, AmeriCorps participants can earn money to apply to college expenses when they are ready to make that transition.

With so many more students applying for college and with so many college options open to students, it can be a real challenge for your teenager to focus on the one college that is right for him. That is why **it is so critically important for your child to spend time thinking and reflecting upon what he wants to get out of the college experience and finding the kind of environment that will bring out the best in him.**

Again, I remind you: one size does NOT fit all! There are a lot of choices in colleges for your child, but the key is to look for the one that will fit him best.

One last thing to remember about the process of finding the right college fit: **The decision about where to go to college can be one of the most important decisions your child has ever had to make.**

Furthermore, this decision has a hefty price tag for which your child probably has no prior frame of reference. Often parents communicate in one way or another to their college-bound children, "For the amount of money we are about to pay or borrow, you better make sure you are making the right choice!" Even though the importance of this decision should not be minimized, we also need to realize the weight and burden this might place upon your child. One of the reasons many college-bound teenagers struggle in making a college choice is the fear of making the wrong one. So at this point on the journey, reassure your child, and yourself, that the choice of which college to attend may not be the "final" one, and that choices can and do change.

I truly believe there is a college for every student who wants to go, but that student has to make the effort to find that college. For some twelfth graders, college will be a natural next step in the months after graduation. Some students, however, need a break and find that taking a year or so off to work or get away from school is just what they need.

Often I meet with students who have been out of high school for a year or more when they conclude, "Now I am ready for college!" When I ask them, "What else could we have done differently for you to see that going to college right out of high school was possible?" They often reply, "Nothing. It was not you, my parents, or even my teachers. I just wanted a break and time away from school. I needed that time to grow up and know for myself that college was something I wanted to do for me, not just something my family and teachers wanted me to do."

A Life of "Right-Fits"

Along the college-bound journey, the keys to

finding the right fit are spending time listening to: 1) your child, 2) high school staff recommendations, and 3) college staff at the institutions your child is interested in. This process of discerning, or finding, the right fit takes plenty of time and attention. And finding the "right fit" for college may be an important first for your child, but it will probably not be the last. Finding the right job. Finding the right spouse. Finding the right home. Life is filled with finding the right fit. Take time to help your child navigate this journey now, and he will be much better prepared to navigate future journeys successfully on his own.

Please note: The questions found in Appendices A-E are also available to download and print at www.WithinViewWithinReach.com

Chapter Five Bright Ideas

1. Check out Appendices A-E for important questions to ask yourself, your child, your child's school, and potential colleges.

2. Have an open and honest discussion with your child about his and your readiness to "let go."

3. Assess how well your child responds to prolonged times away from home (such as summer camp) to determine comfort level of attending in-state vs. out-of-state colleges.

4. Look for adequate academic advising services at potential colleges to guide your child while there – especially during the critical freshman year.

5. Consider graduate school connections when looking for the undergraduate college fit.

6. When comparing "public" and "private" colleges make sure you understand what is offered at what costs: tuition, fees, room, board, financial aid options.

7. Talk to parents of college students, college students and recent college graduates to get the "inside scoop."

6

Checking Them Out

To find the right outfit, you need to do some window shopping, some price comparisons and trying on clothes. To find the right college, you need to go on some college tours. College visits, tours, and open houses are your opportunity to "kick the tires," see the facilities at their best, and get a feel for the place. But many families wonder: "Should we even bother visiting a college we know we cannot afford?" At a minimum, the experience of visiting a college campus exposes you to the fuller scope of what is available to your child in the various price ranges.

You might also think of a college visit as test driving a new car. When we are considering buying a new car, we read about different vehicles, talk to car owners, family and friends, look at all the advertisements, devour the manufacturer's web site, and even go to the dealership to take a test drive. In reality, the car is way out of our price range. So why are we more willing to invest the time and energy to check out a car than we are a priceless college education? Obviously, your child's education is much more important and precious than any vehicle. Additionally, the resources to make the "dream" of a college education a reality are more readily available. So why not check them out?

The "Long List" for College Visits

Once you and your child identify the colleges that may be an appropriate fit, make a long list for possible college visits. Many colleges offer several ways through which you can gain first hand information and insight into their college experience: information sessions, tours, and Open Houses. During information sessions, which last approximately one hour, college admissions officers present vital information about the school's student body, curriculum, campus life, and unique qualities. These sessions may provide important financial aid information and a brief time for questions and answers. Campus tours, which are usually offered in conjunction with the information sessions, are often led by currently enrolled students to expose you to the campus life including classrooms, student housing, dining amenities, and athletic facilities. Additionally, during your campus tours, you and your child can interface directly, and more intimately, with a student to ask more personal questions about their experience to get more insight from a student's perspective.

Many colleges also offer "Open Houses" in the fall and spring, a day where the school rolls out the red carpet for potential students. During Open Houses, many schools have brief presentations by campus notables, including chancellors, distinguished professors, Nobel Laureates, and NCAA champion coaches and players. Generally, Open Houses are free or have a minimal charge to cover the cost of parking and lunch. Occasionally, colleges include tickets to sporting events in conjunction with the Open House, offering multiple ways to expose your child to the wealth of academic, cultural and social resources the college offers and to make him feel at home.

In my own experience, the Open Houses offered in the fall are often more relaxed and easier to navigate than the spring events. During the fall, most of the potential students and their parents are more curious and less intense, and the current college students are more rested and ready to show you their college home. In the spring, visiting families are more eager and aggressive since more eleventh and twelfth grade students are closer to making their final decision or they have been wait-listed and are hoping to make a final appeal to the

Admissions Office. Also, high school spring breaks give families in the US and overseas a concentrated time in March and April to descend on college campuses.

To find out procedures for and availability of campus tours and Open Houses, go to the college's web site or call the Admissions Office. In most instances, you can find tour information by clicking "Undergraduate Admissions," "Prospective Students," "Future Students," "Visiting Campus," "Campus Tours," or "Directions" on the school's home page. However, if this information is not immediately available, type the following in the "Search" box: Open House, Tours, College Visits. If you are still unable to find the information using the "Search" function, then call the Admissions Office using the number usually listed at the bottom of the home page, and ask them directly for dates and times available for college tours. You may also wish to ask if there is a specific admissions officer who is the contact person for your state, region, county, or country.

Specialized Open Houses

Nowadays, individual college departments and professional associations will also conduct Open Houses, tours, and career days to promote who they are and what they offer to prospective students. Some professional schools at universities (such as a School of Pharmacy or School of Engineering) conduct Open Houses and tours to promote specific programs to prospective students as well. These specialized Open Houses give additional insight to high school students who want to know more about specific careers and majors to help them become better prepared for acceptance into what may be highly competitive programs.

Some colleges also offer "recruitment" events to attract and "get" the students they want. Recruitment events are an "all hands on deck" affair. Many recruitment events involve admissions personnel, alumni, administrators, and athletes to communicate loud and clear, "This is who we are, and this is why we want you!" Colleges spend millions of dollars strategizing about how to recruit and retain the students they desire. They produce events, brochures, commercials and web sites to make the message clearer. These schools are very genuine in their efforts, however, remember, these events are definitely "infomercials" that are intended to show you and your child the best of what they have to offer without revealing the multiple challenges and obstacles of surviving college life.

Find Out the "Real Deal"

Since the events described above are clearly designed to show you the "best side" of the school, you must do your homework to ask the "real" questions that need to be answered. Every college and every college student has challenges, and you need to check out how the school helps your child respond to those challenges. Who will be there to help your child when he gets his first bad grade or gets a severe case of strep throat and you are not there to nurse him back to health? These are the kind of questions that you should consider before the need actually arises. When you and your child check out a college or university, ask about what they offer in Residential Assistance, Student Health Services, and Academic Advising. When visiting a campus whether virtually online, through a catalog, or on a campus tour find out about their Resident Assistance Program or "RAs," as they are often called. The RA will often be the person to whom your child goes because he is having a problem with a roommate or is struggling in the classroom. Each school should provide strong staff who are ready and able to respond to multiple scenarios to help your child both survive and thrive once he gets to college. Likewise, most students are assigned academic advisors, university staff who can help them navigate course selection, tutorial assistance, declaring a major and most importantly meeting graduation requirements.

When They Come to You

But what if your child is interested in a school too far from home to make a campus visit? Colleges understand that not all families have the funds or interest to participate in an Open House or tour. So, as a kind of "short cut," they send their "show on the road" by offering regional information sessions. Many colleges send representatives, either staff from the Admissions Office or local alumni, to make presentations to interested students and families. **To find out if a college is offering information sessions in your area, check out the college's web site.** Bear in mind, many colleges have downsized their travel budgets and outreach efforts due to financial pressures. As a result, more and more colleges are sending alumni to do information sessions and now even offer prospective student interviews via internet. The purpose of the regional information sessions is to give you and your child a "friendly face" from the university to help you become familiar and more comfortable with the college or university.

Combined College Events

Another increasingly common event being offered is the combined college information session. To maximize resources and cut down on costs, many colleges are hosting combined college information sessions where multiple colleges come together to provide information about their school through panel presentations. For instance, in one event held at a hotel in North Carolina, representatives from Harvard, Duke, and the University of Pennsylvania presented to interested families and prospective students on a Sunday evening.

In these combined sessions, each school admissions representative provides a short overview often accompanied by a video or slide presentation followed by a general question and answer session. Following the presentations, the school representatives are then available to interested students and families to answer more direct questions about their respective institutions. Often times, the colleges will combine this type of event with informational sessions for local high school counselors.

Another common means to check out various schools are college fairs. At college fairs, many colleges gather in one place for one or more days in a community to promote the schools to students in the area. In our community in North Carolina, Elon University hosts the CACRAO college fair in the school's gymnasium. Over two days, more than seventy colleges display information and provide representatives from their Admissions Offices who are present to answer brief questions and talk with prospective students. **To find out if a college fair is scheduled for your area, visit the National Association for College Admission Counseling web site (www.nacacnet.org) or the web site of your local public school system which often advertises these events.**

Ask the Alumni

As mentioned earlier, college alumni can be a wealth of information and connections for your child. Therefore, look for local college alumni association chapter meetings of interest for you and your child to attend. A few years ago, North Carolina State University sponsored a local alumni luncheon in our community to which interested students were invited. At my encouragement, a local high school student attended the event, and while there, connected so successfully that he was offered a scholarship to an academic summer camp sponsored at the school. To find out about local alumni chapter meetings, check out the college's web site or alumni association chapter's web site to find dates, times, and locations of local meetings. If a date for a local chapter meeting is not listed, contact the university alumni association about alumni contacts and events in your area.

Up Close and Personal

If your child is ready to take the next step in checking out a particular college, **you can arrange for your child to take an overnight visit on campus.** Generally, overnight visits can be arranged through the school's admissions office. Or if you or your child know a current college student you can trust at the school, plan for him to spend a night or two on campus where he can explore and experience campus life up close and personal: attending class, eating meals, socializing, meeting people.

Another interesting way to explore more in depth what a school has to offer is for your child to **sit in on a class at the college.** At most colleges, you will need to obtain permission from the admissions office or from a department administrator. However, this extra effort provides a great opportunity to get a feel for the classroom and instruction and the level of interaction between students and faculty. In some cases, a professor may share his syllabus or send you to the department's web site to look more closely at the curriculum.

For some students, the "right" school will have the extracurricular activities they desire. If this is your child, **spend time exploring information about the various clubs and extracurricular activities a college offers.** For instance, if your child is interested in playing in the marching band, your child should try to connect with a current student who is participating in this part of campus life to find out their satisfaction with the experience. Also visit the department to find out the requirements to be in marching band such as tryouts, number of hours required to practice per week, cost of uniforms, and travel. Additionally, if your child likes what he hears, applies to the college, and is accepted, he has a connection as he enters life on campus.

Summer Camps on College Campuses

One way to get your child to consider "checking out" a school is to get them on campus for something that really interests them. **Summer academic and athletic camps offer unique glimpses of campus life while immersing your child in an activity of their choice.** Over the past few years, I had been meeting with a family about college prospects for their son. He was a great student who also happens to be a basketball player. While he was perfectly comfortable traveling abroad and checking out schools all over his home state of North Carolina, he had a hard time taking seriously our suggestions of checking out Ivy League schools. So, last summer I suggested to him that he check out Harvard's basketball camp in hopes that his love for basketball would get him there and that being immersed on Harvard's campus would do the rest. As it turns out, the basketball camp was less expensive than the local camp he had attended in previous years – including his airfare to Boston! Sure enough, this "no way I'm going there" attitude shifted to "OK, I'll give it a try." As a result, this student enjoyed the camp but enjoyed the school even more. Additionally, his family including his sister who is three years younger, joined him at the end of the week for a college road trip tour that included Princeton and Columbia! For this family, capitalizing on their child's interest in basketball, even if he doesn't play at the college level, opened up a whole new world of possibilities and gave their son a "competitive edge" when making application for other schools of interest including Wake Forest, UNC, Emory, and Oberlin.

The late Kay Yow's girls basketball camp was my first week long overnight college campus experience. I was a rising freshman in high school, and saw how competitive other high school students were, especially those who were pursuing basketball scholarships. The camp was also my first experience of talking with current college athletes about their transition from high school to college and balancing the demands in the classroom and on the court. Additionally, I learned basic college survival skills, such as keeping up with my room keys and money, handling dirty laundry, and getting along with an assigned roommate whom I had just met for the first time.

Checking Them Out from Home

It is possible, at least in part, to check out a college without leaving your home. Many college web sites offer "virtual tours" online and "Satisfaction Survey" results completed by students and parents. But remember, these are often a part of the "marketing" of the school, so they may not give you a complete picture. Additionally, some publications, such as the *US News and World Report*, publish annual reports and "grading" of colleges and universities as well.

So what is the best way to "check out" a school? **Get your child personally involved in the checking!** After all, he will be the one who is ultimately happy – or unhappy – at the school. So the sooner he is involved in assessing the right fit, the better off you both will be. The key to a right fit is often dependent on your child's needs and preferences. So, who better to ask the questions than your child?

Teenagers today often tell me that a campus "feels" right or wrong. This was a new one for me. When I was deciding where to go to college, I did not really need to visit the campus. The pictures in the catalog were pretty, and when I heard "full scholarship" I was sold! But this is not true for most teenagers today. Today's youth are very visual and experiential. They are in search of a certain "feel" about a campus and can usually tell you if they got it on the ride back home.

I strongly recommend that **your child spend time talking to several students attending colleges of interest to him.** At the same time your child is asking questions of other students, you should ask questions of other parents of students at the school. Granted, different folks will have different experiences and therefore will give you different stories. However, the more the input, the more realistic picture you gain of the college.

Checking out schools, like finding the right fit, can be mind-boggling. As you sift through mounds of brochures, web sites, conversations, and tours,

the best way to get it all in focus is to focus on your child's and your priorities. These priorities might include academic major/field of study, extracurricular activities, housing options, distance from home and affordability. In the next chapter, we explore how to count the costs to prioritize what is most important in your child's choice of college. **To help you and your child sort through all the information, keep a notebook of the colleges of most interest to you.** Assess how well each school meets these top priorities then rank each school by choice.

Of course, as with buying a new car, even all the consumer reports and hard data cannot substitute for how it "feels" and "fits." So keep asking the questions, keep visiting web sites and campuses, and keep interfacing with others who have experienced the school firsthand. Once you start to seriously check them out, preferably by the sophomore year, you can narrow down the "long list" to the "short list" of schools that meet your top priorities and provide the best fit for your child and his academic needs.

Chapter Six Bright Ideas

1. Make a "long list" of colleges that may be an appropriate fit for possible college visits.

2. Check out a college's web site under "Admissions" to find the available campus tours and open houses.

3. Be prepared to ask in-depth questions to discover the "real them" that goes beyond a college's "best side."

4. Ask every college about their Residential Assistance and Academic Advising services for students – especially services and programs for freshman or first year students.

5. Check out a college's web site to see if they are offering information sessions in your local area.

6. To find out about college fairs in your area, check out the web sites for National Association for College Admission Counseling (www.nanacnet. org) and your local public school system.

7. Look for local college alumni association chapter meetings.

8. Arrange for an overnight visit on campus for your child if he decides he is serious about a school.

9. Check out the extracurricular options of interest to your child.

10. Encourage your child to attend an athletic or

academic summer camp on a college campus.

11. Talk to other students and parents of students who currently attend a school of interest.

12. Keep a notebook of your child's "top choices" with a checklist of how each meets his "top priorities."

7

Counting the Costs

"We don't have the money."** Many students never even consider some viable college options, much less complete an application for admission, because they assume certain college choices are not realistic for them. Granted, the cost of going to college can be a real obstacle for many families. **But before you rule out any school, you need to assess the actual costs and find what resources are potentially available.**

Involve Your Child

Counting the cost and setting a budget for the college-bound journey is a prime opportunity to involve your child in what is required to invest in and fulfill his future. For many students, preparing a college budget is the first time they have established priorities, assessed costs, set a budget, and then found the resources to make it happen. Your child should not be expected to do this without your help. However, this is the perfect chance to equip your teenager in this essential skill he will need throughout his life.

Additionally, if you fail to involve your teenager in this important step of budgeting on the college-bound journey, your child will have no sense of what things cost or his responsibility for being a wise steward of the money he has while in school. So, to prevent your college-bound student from running through his bank account and yours, **have your child begin to take responsibility for and learn the process of budgeting now while he is still directly under your supervision and under your roof.**

This is especially true if your child has never had a job and has never received a bill in his name. However, all that will change when he receives his first tuition bill or his first financial aid award. These important documents will be addressed in his name from the college he will attend. Every student receives a bill for tuition and fees to be paid. Even if your child is an athlete receiving a full scholarship, there is a bill or account number for your child. It is important for you and your child to understand the tuition bill and financial aid amount in detail. Imagine the excitement – and shock – of learning that you are accepted to college and you already have a bill in your name for thousands of dollars! For many students, this is when their credit history officially begins, and yet they are woefully unprepared for what follows.

The Costs of Exploring and Applying

Before we look at college expenses, let's assess the costs involved in the college exploration and application process. Yes, you also need a budget for costs involved in deciding which school is right for your child! To assess the costs of exploring and applying to colleges, we must look at expenses as early as your child's junior and senior years in high school. **Keep an ongoing checklist of all the things you and your child will need to do in the college exploration process especially during the junior and senior years, and the projected or actual cost of doing them.** As a parent, you may have thought about many of these activities and items, but you have only been keeping them "in your head." However, now is the time to get them down on paper or a computer spreadsheet so that you can clearly calculate the costs and make sure you are not overlooking unexpected expenses. Additionally, this list is not only essential for your knowledge but for your child's knowledge and action as well!

Seven | Counting the Costs

Look in Appendix 7-A to find a budget worksheet for the college exploration and application process. These costs may include travel to colleges of interest, college fairs, summer camps, tutors, coaching to improve interviewing and presentation skills and fees for the SAT or other tests, and college application fees.

Now more than ever, parents are trying to understand, "How do I balance my child's desire to attend a 'big name' school with the sometimes comparable 'big name' price tag?" It is one thing to buy your child the brand name clothes, but it is another thing altogether to spend or borrow tens of thousands of dollars for a college education.

Time Off and Time Out for College Exploration

Parents, whether you are self-employed, unemployed or working three part-time jobs, you need to have a serious talk with yourself, your business partners or supervisors about setting aside several days per year to address college-related matters. I advise parents and students as early as 8th and 9th grade to use teacher workdays, school breaks, and holidays for college tours. At some high schools, college tours are considered "excused absences" especially for juniors and seniors. Take advantage of these opportunities to enjoy a more leisurely paced college tour, possibly on a weekday, when the tour crowds can be smaller. Think about it. With all of the information you and your child are given on college tours, wouldn't the process of visiting and evaluating colleges be so much easier if it was spread out over 2-4 years rather than trying to cram it into six months like many families do. Six months refers to the time from spring break of the 11th grade year to the first semester of the senior year when many families begin the college search in earnest.

Further, if seniors and their parents are not getting timely answers to questions about financial aid, registration, housing, and the like, etc., I advise them to take time off work and school and go to the college to meet face to face with people who have decision-making authority. While some matters can be resolved by phone and e-mail, there are definitely appropriate times when you should make an appointment or take advantage of "no appointment needed" opportunities to get the answers you and your child need from college and university administrators.

Compare the Costs

In reviewing and comparing the price tags for colleges and universities, you quickly realize why

your child should have three or more college choices from which to choose. Four year colleges, private, public, community and technical colleges all offer a variety of class selections and payment options that may factor into your final decision. There are many aspects of the college experience that can be compared dollar for dollar, but there also many intangibles such as status, campus amenities, faculty expertise, research opportunities, and quality of accommodations.

Community colleges offer courses for high school graduates and University Transfer programs in addition to offering classes to high school students for college credit. These institutions now offer options that were not foreseeable twenty-five years ago when community colleges were more limited in scope.

Once you and your child have narrowed down the "best fit" colleges for him, you need to estimate the cost for your child attending each one of the potential schools. Counting the costs involves more than calculating and comparing tuition and housing. First, you need to make sure that you are comparing "apples to apples" and "oranges to oranges." For instance, if you budget $1,000 in spending money for your child, will it go farther in Athens, Georgia (University of Georgia), Palo Alto, California (Stanford University), or College Park,

Maryland (University of Maryland)? Additionally, you need to consider which options will work best for your child and your family, such as starting out the first two years at a community college and transferring to a four year college the junior year.

For many folks, this first look at college expenses is overwhelming. Basically, you are trying to estimate the cost of sending your child to college combined with your continued day-to-day household expenses for the rest of the family at home. This is especially intimidating for families who have no trust funds, very little savings, no Christmas trees planted eighteen years ago waiting to be harvested, and no estate jewelry or family property to be sold. My family would have fallen into this category. For these families, the concept of not knowing exactly how much everything will cost can create quite a panic. For many families living pay check to pay check, the thought of taking loans to fulfill their child's dreams is a "nightmare" they would rather avoid!

Conversely, I have worked with families who started college savings funds before their children were born. These families are just as concerned about protecting their investment and making sure they are getting the best possible value for their dollar, as well as the best possible experience for their child.

Fortunately, most colleges are being more up front and clear about the true costs and expenses by providing an itemized breakdown on the school's web site. **To find the approximate cost of tuition, fees, room and board to attend a school, go to that college's web site and look at the Admissions, Financial Aid, FAQs or At-A-Glance sections for information.**

Factor in Inflation

After obtaining the cost information for each school, calculate the cost factoring inflation for each year that your child will be there. **Check out the web site www.finaid.org and click on the calculator tool to estimate the cost,** including yearly inflation for your child to attend a particular school. As stated on the FinAid web site, the custom calculators "can help you figure out how much school will cost, how much you need to save, and how much aid you'll need."

Make a Budget for Each

Yes, it is a bit frightening to see the actual cost laid out in front of you! But until you can clearly see these figures and bring them *Within View*, it is hard to confirm how much money you need to make your child's dream a reality and bring it *Within Reach*. Once you have fully estimated the hard costs from the perspective of the school, you also need to estimate the OTHER costs associated with getting, and keeping, your child in school, including his physical, intellectual, and social needs. **From Appendix 7-B, complete a cost comparison budget worksheet for each potential college.** It is important to complete the budget worksheet for each potential school since the expenses may vary significantly depending on the cost of tuition, travel expenses, on campus and off campus housing, and the general cost of living.

When completing the budget worksheet for each school, remember to include costs for you and your child to attend orientation the summer before going to college. When my generation was headed to college, our parents simply dropped us off on campus and hung around for a few hours to help us unload and get settled in our rooms. However, that is not true today. The current practice at many colleges is for parents and new students to attend Orientation sessions, which may involve overnight stays on campus. The costs can be potentially prohibitive for some families since it may involve travel, accommodations, and even time away from work.

Another great source of information to estimate

costs is to talk with parents or current students at a particular school. **Talk to parents of current students and ask them what costs they had not estimated, underestimated, or if the financial aid provided was sufficient.**

On the budget worksheet found in Appendix 7-B, you will see a section for "INCOME" and may wonder, "How should I know how much money is available – and from where?!" Again, before you know how much help you need, you need to have a clear idea of the actual costs. Once you have identified the "right fit" and have estimated the cost of attending a "right fit" college, you will need to have the "This is what we are dealing with" conversation as a family. This conversation involves looking closely and honestly at what your family can afford and the resources you will need. In the chapter, "Finding the Resources," we will also discuss where to look and how to obtain the needed resources including grants, scholarships, work study, and loans.

Remember, for many children this may be the first time they have ever participated in frank, open, "adult" conversations about your family's financial assets and liabilities, including your salaries and indebtedness, depending on how much you wish to share. Granted, teenagers have a keen sense of what they "have" or "have not."

Without a doubt, financial status often shows up in the appearance of or lack of designer labels or other coveted items. But this may be the first time your child becomes actively involved in making these financial decisions that will impact the rest of his life. The goal is to empower your child to be a successful part of the team, including assessing, and fulfilling the financial obligations that must be made for college enrollment to run smoothly for your family over the next several years.

Embrace this opportunity of counting and addressing the costs of college TOGETHER with your child. As mentioned earlier, your child needs to be actively involved in estimating and understanding the financial obligations of school, but he should not be expected to do this alone.

I recall one student who chose to leave her home state for a private out of state school. While the parents wanted to support the child's interest and initiative, they were nervous about the financial commitments this choice would require. When a college recruiter found out that the student turned eighteen over the summer, the college informed her that she would no longer need her parents to sign for a loan. It is true that, as an eighteen year old, a student is eligible to take out a loan, but at what cost?

As with any indebtedness, parents and students should exercise great caution when considering how much aid to accept in loans. Debt at any age is a huge burden, but the younger a student incurs debt, the longer and heavier the burden can follow him for years to come if not handled appropriately.

It is always a delight when parents with children in college return to me and say, "We've finally got the hang of this now with the first child in college. It will be much easier with the second one!" Learning how to accurately count the costs and making sure you have the needed resources can be as stressful as the process of supporting your child through the college application and enrollment process.

The cost of college can be more than a car loan, and in some cases, even more than a home mortgage! If you do not have experience with either of these significant financial investments, which is the case for some adults and for most of our children, figuring out how to meet these financial obligations can be very challenging. **The key is in being proactive instead of reactive.** By being proactive, you identify the needs based on the estimated costs so you can have open and honest conversations up front instead of last minute panic attacks when the college bills come due.

Chapter Seven Bright Ideas

1. Check out the real costs and potential resources before you rule out any college choice.

2. Actively involve your child in the budgeting process.

3. Keep a checklist of all the steps and associated costs of the college exploration process.

4. Check out Appendix 7-A for a budget worksheet to estimate costs of the college exploration and application processes.

5. Estimate a budget (using the worksheet in Appendix 7-B) for each of the colleges to which your child is applying.

6. Refer to the college's web site to obtain estimated costs.

7. Check out the college cost calculator tool found at www.finaid.org.

8. Talk to parents of current college students to find out what they underestimated and how much aid they actually needed.

8

Applying to Make it Happen

Now that you have worked with your child to find the right college fit, you have checked the colleges out, and you have counted and compared the costs, it is time for your child to apply to the colleges which are right for him. This is the point on the journey where the "rubber meets the road" to determine the college of choice for your child, and where the college decides if your child is the best choice for them.

The Role of the Admissions Officer

In the same manner you and your child are looking for the best fit for him, Admissions Officers are tasked with finding the best fits to build a solid freshman class in which each student has the best chance to graduate and succeed. Remember: Admissions Officers are graded, too, on how they recruit, present themselves and the university, interact with parents and potential students as well as represent the school at college fairs and alumni events. Their job is a tough one. They are prepared to answer all questions from you and your child, whether he is accepted or not.

In my experience with many colleges, Admissions Officers do their best to examine each application for its own merits and to make what are surely gut-wrenching decisions about who is and is not accepted. Each year, the pool of college applicants is different for each college. Some years the applicant pool is more competitive. Other years, it is less competitive. A student who is admitted to this year's freshman class might not have been accepted in last year's class or even next year's class of admitted freshmen.

Completing the Application

So what are the components that must be completed in the college application? First, there is the application form itself. Some colleges use what is called the "Common Application" which is a common application form used by over 400 colleges including both public and private. The Common Application can be completed online or can be downloaded or completed by hand and mailed as a hard copy. Other colleges have their own specific application which is often completed and submitted online, or it can be completed and mailed as hard copy. **To determine which application to use, go to that college's web site, click on "Admissions," and then follow the instructions for how to apply.**

College Admissions Offices and Scholarship Programs spend incredible resources developing application forms that best ensure they have the information they need to make a well-informed decision about your child. Therefore, your child should **regard the application as "precious real estate" to be treated with great care, and follow the directions closely!**

Whether the application is two or twenty-two pages long, each question and response has been planned meticulously, so your child should use this space well thus the reference to the precious real-estate. Most importantly, make sure that your child follows the directions on the application. Nothing makes application reviewers more inclined to raise serious questions and possibly reject an applicant than seeing that the student did not take the time and energy to read and follow the directions! On any application for college admission or scholarships, make sure that everything is clearly spelled out avoiding any abbreviations and leaving nothing to chance or interpretation.

Completing Any Supplements

Some colleges that use the Common Application also require your child to complete a supplement that is specific to that college. Again, this will be clearly indicated on the college's web site, so follow their instructions and checklist for applying. Most applications whether Common or specific have various sections to be completed, including contact information, future plans, demographics, family/parent information, academics, test scores, and activities. Again, your child should complete each section thoroughly and accurately, paying close attention to avoid typographical errors or omissions. To ensure your child has completed the application in a thorough manner, **ask your child if you or another trusted adult can proofread and review any parts of the entire application before it is submitted.**

Writing the Essays

As part of the application form, sometimes your child will be asked to complete a personal essay. This is where your child can really shine. Personal essays are the "freebie" part of the application where your child can talk about what has shaped him into who he is and what he wants to become. Remember: **the essay is the primary means by**

which the school is "interviewing" your child on paper to determine how they will fit in and what they will contribute to the university community. Too often, students are so focused on getting into the most competitive colleges so they try to make their scholarship profiles "fit" what the Admissions Officers or donors want to hear. However, this cab be a big mistake. What Admission Officers and scholarship application readers are looking for is what motivates this applicant as characterized by their experiences, their activities, and their observations as outlined in the application and essay.

In fact, if your child is later called for a face-to-face interview, application readers and interviewers will be listening to see if your child's personality on paper mirrors the student in person. As mentioned earlier, in addition to your child's grades and academic performance, the college wants to know about his passion and pursuits. They want to know how he will make a difference on their campus in traditional and non-traditional ways. For many students, this type of in-depth self-reflection does not come naturally and may require some time to prepare. Therefore, **encourage your child to take time during his eleventh grade year and the summer before his senior year to begin constructing the personal essay.** As mentioned earlier, make sure that your child has you or another trustworthy and experienced adult proofread the essay before sending it in!

The Transcript

Another key piece of your child's application is his transcript or summary of academic work and performance at his current school. Again, follow the instructions on the college's application, but most often this form can be downloaded and completed from the web site. **The "Official Transcript" will be completed and sent in by your child's guidance counselor or college advisor.**

I get looks of surprise when I explain to ninth, tenth and eleventh graders that the grades on their high school transcript at the end of the junior year are the grades that colleges will see if they apply to college in September or October of their senior year. Here's what I mean: most students will not have their first nine weeks grades on their transcript until November of the senior year. The classes they are enrolled in for first semester of the senior year will be listed **but not the grades.** Senior year classes and grades are important and the "Final Transcript" issued at the end of the senior year is critical. In reality though, college and scholarship application readers will have in front of them your child's performance in grades nine through eleven.

If nothing else, this should give your child even more motivation to stay focussed the last two years of high school.

Obtaining Letters of Recommendation

In addition to the personal essay, the letters of recommendation or reference from teachers and others give a glimpse into the student's home life, work ethic, dreams and habits. **In selecting who should write letters of recommendation, you need to ask, "Who can help tell my child's story?"** For many colleges and scholarship committees, letters of recommendation are required or strongly recommended. Review carefully the criteria for whom the college requests to write these letters. Some colleges require at least one of the letters to be from a teacher or instructor who taught your child and others may require a person from the community other than a teacher. The letters of recommendation serve as a type of "third party assessment" that helps the application reader understand better how your child processes information, responds to his environment, including adversity, takes on new challenges, and prepares for career aspirations.

Sometimes, students select persons with fancy titles, lots of money, or those who would be described as "VIPs." The thinking behind such a selection is that such a person's name and credentials would carry the weight needed to get an absolute "YES" from the Admissions Committee. Although this could be a safe assumption, too many of these letters make it abundantly clear that the writer knows the parents well but not the student applicant. In contrast, a lesser known person without fancy titles, credentials, or money may have the breadth and depth of knowledge about your child and your family's successes and failures, mountains and valleys, to communicate your child's ability to weather challenges and positively impact others. The most important criteria for selecting who writes your child's letter of recommendation is this: **Select the person who knows your child best and can best communicate the unique contributions of your child.**

Most importantly, make sure that the person who writes the letter of recommendation is a reasonably good writer who can tell your child's story. On occasion, I have read letters of recommendation in which the writer did not know the student well or may not have had the selection criteria available to know how the student was being evaluated. Sometimes, unfortunately, they are poor writers. At times, a student asks a teacher who is unsure, or even unsupportive, of the student. Or these less than helpful letters may also be the result of a last minute request that did not allow the writer adequate time to prepare.

Unfortunately, many students do not really think about who they will ask to write their letters of recommendation until days – or even hours – before they need them! If you want a letter writer to have enough time to study and respond appropriately to the selection criteria, begin talking with your child during the junior year about possible teachers, coaches, youth counselors, or employers who could write these letters. **To obtain the "best" letters of recommendation in the most timely manner, identify the letter writers the summer before your child's senior year and have your child ask them soon enough to prepare.**

When requesting a letter of recommendation, your child should prepare a short memo to the prospective writer which should let them know the following: a list of colleges to which your child is applying; a list of scholarships for which your child is applying; a link to or copy of directions for the letters of recommendations for each college or scholarship including word limit, required font, and selection criteria; a resume to include your child's school activities, awards, community activities, leadership positions, summer activities, employment, or other experiences and interests;

a transcript which may or may not include SAT or ACT scores making sure to highlight any advanced classes or college credits; a list of other persons your child is asking to write letters of recommendation.

To assist families, applicants, teachers and others in writing letters of recommendations, some colleges will send you instructions and samples of exemplary recommendation letters.

Telling the Whole Story

Letters of recommendation can serve to describe how exemplary your child is but they also can serve to explain some of your child's shortcomings, weaknesses and bad decisions. During my freshman year at the University of North Carolina, the late Richardson Pryer, former United States Congressman, was my teacher in "Legislative Ethics," the course in which I received my first "C." I was interested in taking the class which would be limited to about twenty students but I was disappointed to learn that it was for seniors and first year law students. Given my interest in politics, I thought it would be a once in a lifetime opportunity to take a class with such a decorated congressman. So, I talked my way into the class after visiting personally with Congressman Pryer, despite my academic advisor's advice not to take the class because it would be too challenging for a freshman. As you might guess, I greatly overestimated my ability to do well in the class. Even though I was disappointed in making a "C," I had a great time hearing the stories of a decorated and sage congressman and experiencing class with seniors and law school students.

When I went to see Congressman Pryer at the end of the semester, as I did with most of my professors, he was very complimentary about how well I had done in the classroom discussions and debates, especially given that my classmates were three to four years older than I. He pointed out that given time and experience, my writing would improve. And he even encouraged me to pursue a career in law and politics!

Years later, as a senior, when I was preparing applications for law school and the Rhodes scholarship, I believed that: 1) the "C" on my transcript would require an explanation and 2) I needed a letter from someone who could talk about my freshman year performance and how I had challenged myself and progressed at UNC. So, I chose Congressman Pryer to help me tell my story. He had kept up with my career at Carolina and gladly wrote the letter. Had I not taken the opportunity to talk with him at the end of the semester, and had I not openly discussed my academic strengths and weakness with him and received his criticism, he would not have been as effective a witness and writer of my story in the letter of recommendation.

Explaining the Use of Time

When I sit on application and scholarship review committees, I want to understand how a student uses his time in and out of the classroom. I can get a glimpse of that on forms, but the essay and letters of recommendation shed more light and give texture to who the student really is and what they are able to contribute. By looking at the fuller picture, such as the answers on the application forms, the personal essays, the letters of recommendations, the transcript, and the extracurricular activities, these give me insight into how well the student performs both in and outside the classroom.

Your child's application should reflect how he chooses to spend his time. From the transcript, you can determine the coursework demand. From the extracurricular activities, you get a glimpse of a student's passion and commitment to a sport, the arts, or the community. Even if a student works ten or forty hours a week to contribute to the family's finances, this reflects his commitment to support the greater needs of the family.

Often high school students who must work to support other dependents or to contribute to the household budget think they will not be competitive for merit-based scholarships because they did not participate in as many extracurricular activities. However, the opposite could be true. Assuming a student's grades are strong, he makes good test scores, and has strong letters of recommendations and a personal essay that tells his story well, he may be just as competitive as the student with a long list of activities but demonstrates little initiative at contributing to the family's or community's greater good.

Keep Hard Copies

With the ability to submit applications online, we often forget to keep hard copies. As a safeguard and backup, **print hard copies of all the completed forms, confirmation sheets, and a full copy of the completed college application before or after you hit "submit" to file online.** While electronic submissions are certainly easier, it is still critically important to keep copies of everything in the event something gets lost or misplaced in the process of applying. I have seen many students and parents panic when they receive a letter or e-mail from a college stating that the application or a particular document had not been received. Likewise, make copies and keep a file folder of all documents sent by U.S. mail, courier, or even by e-mail to create a paper trail of all documents submitted.

Conducting Interviews

On occasion, some colleges will contact your child for an interview to supplement the written application. While some colleges regard the prospective student interviews a typical part of the application process, many schools do not require or initiate interviews. Additionally, with the increased cost of travel, many schools do not require on site interviews but rather may arrange for your child to interview with a local alumnus in your area or even to interview over the phone.

As mentioned earlier in this chapter, the personal essay is, in fact, the "first interview." Therefore, anything that your child says in a face-to-face or phone interview should reflect the same message of who he is and what he is about. **To help your child be ready for interviews, prepare possible interview questions and practice with him. Also, ask a trusted adult who will give him honest, constructive criticism to conduct a "mock interview."**

"Need-Blind" Applications

Again, let me remind you that your child's decision whether or not to apply to a school should not be limited to whether or not you think your family can afford it. **College Admissions Officers do not know if you have money to pay for college or not.** Their job is to find the most competitive and best-suited applicants to create an interesting and successful freshman class. In the application itself, such as your child's essay or reference letters from other individuals, the Admissions Officer may see evidence that your family has encountered financial hardships or obstacles, but that would not be the focus of the Admissions Officer.

In some instances, Admissions Officers are tasked with recommending certain applicants for merit or need-based scholarships based on certain criteria. Otherwise, the work of the Admissions Officers in reviewing applications is what is deemed "need blind," or the reviewer is "blind" to the applicant's financial need or ability to pay.

For the overwhelming majority of students receiving a "Congratulations! You have been accepted" letter from the College Admissions Office, the discussion about ability to pay begins when your child receives that first packet of information from the college's Office of Financial Aid. However,

I do want to be realistic that some colleges do give preference in the admissions process to students based on their family's current or past giving record or donations to the school. Higher education is a competitive business!

Even though financial information is not a direct part of the application process, there are ways to reveal that information such as in the essays or letters of recommendation as mentioned earlier. This allows the applicant or person writing a letter of recommendation to talk about a wide range of experiences which might include evidence of financial need, housing situations, overcoming adversity

Pay Attention to Deadlines

Another key thing to consider in submitting the application is **WHICH DEADLINE** does your child want to follow? All deadlines are not the same, and which deadline you choose to follow determines when your child will be notified and may impact other decisions with other schools. Check carefully the application, financial aid and scholarship deadlines of each college and determine which deadline is right for your child with each school.

There are often at least three types of deadlines,

and each one has different implications for each college. So look at the college's web site to determine which deadline is right for your child in each circumstance. Types of deadlines may include:

Early decision, which is often a "binding commitment" to attend this school if your child is accepted. Your child should choose early decision for ONLY ONE COLLEGE which represents his first choice. Early decision allows your child to apply and find out early in the senior year if they are admitted.

Early action, which is usually a "non-binding commitment" allows your child to learn of the admission decision early in the senior year but without committing your child to attend if accepted.

Regular decision, which is a "non-binding commitment" if accepted, allows your child to submit his application under regular deadlines and to find out the admission decision usually in winter or early spring of his senior year.

Whereas your child can only apply "early decision" to one school, the school which is his first choice, he should apply regular decision or early action if possible to other schools he is considering. This also allows for a contingency plan in the event that he is not accepted to his first choice school.

One final piece of advice about completing the application: **If you or your child have questions or concerns regarding any part of the application or process, contact the Admissions Office or scholarship program in charge of the application.** It is better to be clear on what information they want than to be embarrassed about calling. Your child's willingness to get the information he needs to complete the application only demonstrates his willingness and commitment to follow-through on tasks.

Completing and submitting the application is often the most nerve-wracking part of the journey for your child. Therefore, it can be very nerve-wracking for you. The key to submitting a "successful" application is having your child, and the information you need, prepared and ready to put it all together. So begin as early as possible. File each piece away. Keep copies of everything. Review each piece before sending. Then, after much thought and prayer, send it on its way!

Chapter Eight Bright Ideas

1. Go to the web site of each college under "Admissions" to find the specific application to be completed and deadlines.

2. Treat the application as "precious real estate" to be completed accurately and completely.

3. Make sure that you or another trusted adult proofread and review all parts of the application packet before your child submits it.

4. Encourage your child to begin work on his personal essay by the summer before his senior year or even during his junior year.

5. Select and ask the person(s) who can best "tell your child's story" to write a letter of recommendation well in advance.

6. Print hard copies and keep a file of all forms, essays, and documents submitted as part of the application.

7. Prepare interview questions and practice mock interviews with your child and/or ask other experienced adults to assist you with this.

8. Select the appropriate deadline for each school working from your child's first choice school.

9. Contact the Admission Office with any questions regarding the application form or process.

9

Finding the Resources

As mentioned in the previous chapter, applying to and waiting for acceptance from your child's college of choice is often the most nerve-wracking part of the college-bound journey for your child. Parents and students are both ecstatic when that acceptance letter comes. For your child, he often thinks, "Wow, the tough part is done!" But for you, the "tough part" is just beginning. Now you have to find the resources to get him and keep him in college over the next four or more years.

A few weeks after receiving the coveted acceptance letter from Harvard, I received a phone call from the Harvard Financial Aid office. The very nice lady kindly told me how much money my family would need to pay for me to come to Harvard. I remember asking about scholarships, but during the 1980s at the Ivies the conventional thought was "loans, loans and more loans". After all, it was Harvard! For my family with two younger brothers also college-bound, borrowing that much money was not a viable option. So at that point Harvard seemed less likely a possibility. When I told my dad the amount of money the nice lady at Harvard said I would need to enroll there, his response was "That cost more than our house." As a seventeen year old in 1981 it was my first meaningful understanding of how much college could cost – "as much as a house."

There are times when the college of your child's dreams may seem out of reach financially. However, **never make the determination that a college is out of reach financially until you first ask, seek and find the answers that you need.**

With a full athletic scholarship to Duke and a full academic scholarship to UNC-Chapel Hill in hand, I no longer considered Harvard a realistic option. However, within two weeks of receiving the call from Harvard's financial aid office I received a phone call from Alex Haley, the late author of *Roots*. Mr. Haley had done genealogical research in my hometown as he wrote the book. I met him my senior year in high school and he knew of my interest in Harvard. Mr. Haley told me Harvard had informed him of my acceptance and how much money I needed to attend. Then, like magic, he said, "If you decide you want to go to Harvard, I'll pay for it. All four years." For one of the first times in my life, I would make a decision about my future, and money would not be the primary consideration.

Ask to Find

This is often the point on the journey where families, especially parents, feel most "exposed" or vulnerable. Telling the college's financial aid office about your family's economic situation, which may include talking about family illness, economic hardship, job loss, or divorce, can be very difficult. Sometimes families view this part of the process as "begging." However, when you state your case to receive financial aid or request financial assistance, you are not "begging." Challenging and changing family situations abound from the business owner who had to file for bankruptcy, to families moving from gated communities to rent-controlled apartments, to teenage moms living in homeless shelters. None of us want to feel embarrassed about our financial or home situations. But to receive the financial assistance available, you must state your case honestly and openly.

The college's financial aid officers are there to assist you and your child to get the help you need. They are not there to keep your child out of college! Instead, they have the tough job of helping you and others complete the legal documents needed to make decisions about your child's financial eligibility for various types of help. **The key is to document your story and your need as clearly as possible. And don't wait until the last minute to ask for help!**

Paying Your Part

For better or for worse, there is an expectation on the part of most colleges and the government that families should contribute to their child's education without enduring severe hardship. With the recent decline in our nation's economy, many families who had previously intended to pay cash for their child's college education are now finding those resources depleted or gone. While the government attempts to provide continued Pell grants for the lowest income families, university endowments all over the nation have been hit hard with dwindling resources to help students. As a result, families are being expected to work harder than ever to find additional funding to pay for their child's education.

On many occasions, I have met parents who are financially strapped and struggle to pay for the basics of daily family life. In other instances, I work with families who make just a little "too much" money to qualify for fee waivers and other financial assistance, yet they are challenged to come up with the funds needed for application fees, test fees, and the like.

In anger and frustration, I have had many a parent ask me, "Why do we have to fill out so many forms? We are barely making it." For so long, many families have thought that if their child just made good grades, there would be plenty of scholarships for their child to go to college for free. However, times are changing. With more people applying to college and college expenses rising at rapid rates, families and students must be willing to work hard, to sacrifice time and resources, and to hunt for the money aggressively.

Completing the FAFSA

In spite of this seemingly disparaging word, there are many resources available if you are willing to do the work of finding them. Resources to pay for college come in several categories including scholarships, grants, work study, and loans. For most students, the student financial aid package from the college where your child is accepted will include some combination of many, if not all, of these.

Complete the Free Application for Federal

Student Aid (FAFSA) form as a first step in finding available government resources. The FAFSA, produced by the U.S. Department of Education, is a free application using your tax information and other personal data that you complete in order for the government to determine your child's eligibility to receive grants ("free money"), loans (money which must be repaid), and work-study employment (a job, usually on campus, which allows the student to receive a paycheck to offset fees payable for the semester).

Go to the U.S. Department of Education web site: www.fafsa.ed.gov to find the information you need to complete the FAFSA.

Many families mistakenly believe that the FAFSA is a loan application or is a commitment to borrow money. This is absolutely not true! You can think about completing the FAFSA form like getting "pre-qualified" for a mortgage or car loan. The FAFSA allows the federal government to tell you how much federal funding or financial aid assistance you and your child can expect to receive as well as how much you will be expected to contribute, or the Expected Family Contribution (EFC).

To determine the EFC, the government uses a formula that factors in the student's income (and assets, if the student is independent), the parents' income and assets (if the student is dependent), the family's household size, and the number of family members (excluding parents) attending postsecondary institutions. An estimated figure of how much your family should be able to contribute to your child's college education is calculated based on a percentage of your net family income (after basic living expenses) and a percentage of your assets. Once the government has determined your EFC, a report is sent both to you (a Student Aid Report or SAR) and to the college (an Institutional Student Information Report or ISIR).

While it is recommended that you complete your taxes BEFORE you complete the FAFSA, you can still get assistance in completing the form before your taxes are filed. **Many states offer families a FAFSA Day or free ongoing FAFSA assistance provided by financial aid professionals who will help you complete the document online.** FAFSA also offers families the chance to get an early glimpse into their financial aid eligibility before applying to specific colleges. **Get an early estimate of your eligibility for federal student aid by going to the FAFSA4caster web site www.fafsa4caster. ed.gov to learn about the financial aid process.**

To complete the FAFSA form yourself, or when you call to get assistance from others, review the FAFSA Checklist found in Appendix 9-A to make sure that you have the needed information readily available.

Who Files the FAFSA

According to FAFSA, "parent" refers to the biological or adoptive parent of the student. See www.fafsa.ed.gov. Grandparents, foster parents, legal guardians, older siblings, aunts, or uncles are NOT considered parents on the FAFSA form unless they have adopted the student. In the case of divorce or separation, the student is asked to give information about the parent with whom he has lived the most in the past twelve months. If the student did not live with one parent any more than the other, then he is asked to provide information on the parent who provided the most financial support during the past twelve months. If the divorced parent has remarried, the student is also asked to provide information about the stepparent.

If you have acted as the student's legal guardian but are not a parent, it is critically important to have a frank, open discussion regarding who will be financially responsible for college expenses. Even if you have been the primary care provider, you cannot complete the FAFSA for the student unless you meet the criteria outlined in the FAFSA form. In the event this is the case and the student's parents are not able or willing to take financial responsibility for the college expenses, the student may need to pursue legal advice or "emancipation" so he can file the FAFSA as an independent.

Determining Financial Aid Award

On the FAFSA form, you and your teenager will be asked to include the codes for up to eight colleges so that your child can be considered for funding through various sources. Each college and code number you list will receive a copy of the FAFSA report for your child. The FAFSA information received by each college you designate will then be used to develop the "financial aid award" for your child.

When you are completing the FAFSA form you will notice **there is a link to find the codes for each college. Once you find them, you may want to record the college code before completing the FAFSA so you will have them readily available if needed again.**

Estimated Family Contribution

Whether your child is going to Harvard, Howard, or Hertford Community College, the EFC will be the same. The EFC is the government's estimate of how much you are expected to contribute given the information you have provided on the FAFSA form. However, some parents get this confused. They think that the more expensive the college the more funding they will receive from the government. Sometimes they think, the less money the family has, the more money their child automatically receives. **However, the EFC is calculated without consideration of the actual cost of a particular college.** For this reason, the sooner you complete the FAFSA and receive the EFC, the clearer the picture becomes regarding how much money your child needs in order to attend each college.

Families are often surprised when I tell them that thousands of dollars in financial aid are only available **AFTER** their child is accepted to a specific college. In other words, you may never know what scholarship dollars are available to attend a certain college until your child applies and is accepted to that school. At that point, once you have completed the FAFSA and the school receives that information, then more funds may be made available through that specific school as outlined in your child's financial aid package.

On the other hand, some higher income families make the mistake of assuming that there is no need to complete the FAFSA because their child will not be eligible for financial assistance. **Regardless of your income, complete the FAFSA to maximize your child's ability to receive as much funding as possible.** Even though a higher income family may be able to foot most or all of the bill, why not apply to see what assistance is available? Applying for financial aid is similar to the sentiment expressed on a billboard advertising the lottery: Chances of winning the lottery if you don't play? ZERO!"

Scholarships

Once you have completed the FAFSA, you should continue to **look for assistance available through scholarships.** Again, scholarships provide "free money" to students based on their excellence in academics, athletics, leadership abilities, or other achievements. Scholarships are awarded by a large number of organizations ranging from colleges to churches to community organizations and corporations. Some students start as early as tenth or eleventh grade to identify possible scholarships.

While there are some scholarships that "find you," many scholarships out there are waiting to be found by you! One of the best places to begin the scholarship search is in your own community. Many churches, places of worship, community organizations, and employers offer scholarships to local students. **If your child's school has an annual Awards Day for graduating seniors, look at the printed program from years past to identify companies, foundations, or organizations that sponsored scholarships for local students.** Also, check the web site of your local school system to find potential scholarships. You can apply directly for some of these scholarships. Some recipients are selected by the school or a scholarship committee. In either case, find out about any scholarships listed and ask about selection criteria and how to apply.

In my experience, the students who receive the most scholarships begin searching seriously at least by their junior year. To find the amazing abundance of scholarships out there, you also have to be willing to think and look "outside the box." For instance, the North Carolina Blueberry Growers Association sponsors an essay scholarship every year… and you don't even have to like blueberries!

While there are millions of dollars in scholarship monies available on countless web sites, some scholarships are only available to students accepted to particular institutions and who meet certain eligibility requirements. Some colleges have restricted and unrestricted funds or gifts from alumni, corporations, or other friends of the college which can be used to assist students in numerous ways such as paying for tuition, room and board, travel abroad, books, purchase of lap tops, or other essential materials, like a coat.

A recent informational DVD from Harvard tells the story of an alumnus from India who had a specific need to be filled while she was a freshman. When the student moved to Harvard (Boston) from the "extreme south" (India), she found that she was not prepared for that first cold winter. In response to her need, she learned of a winter coat scholarship that had been established to assist students from "the south" who had needs at Harvard. And so, she applied for the scholarship and received the money to meet her specific need!

When I applied to and was accepted to Harvard, I was amazed at the number and diversity of scholarship offerings ranging from students who were from a specific county in Montana to students who played the violin. Unfortunately, at that point, Harvard did not offer specific scholarships for female athletes, African Americans, students from small textile towns in the south, or ones aspiring to be corporate lawyers. The bottom line regarding scholarships is this: **You will never know what is available until you look for it and apply for it. In other words, you must SEEK before you will FIND!**

Another key factor in finding scholarship money

is MOTIVATION. For me, I had a lot of incentive to look for the resources because I knew scholarships would be the only way my family would ever afford for me, and my two brothers, to get to college.

Work Study

Another potential source of financial assistance for your child is work study. The US Department of Education defines the Federal Work Study (FWS) Program as:

The Federal Work Study Program *provides funds that are earned through part-time employment to assist students in financing the cost of postsecondary education. Students can receive FWS funds at approximately 3,400 participating postsecondary institutions. Institutional financial aid administrators at participating institutions have substantial flexibility in determining the amount of FWS awards to provide to students who are enrolled or accepted for enrollment. Hourly wages must not be less than the federal minimum wage.*

In conversations with many parents, I have heard a range of responses about whether or not their child should have a job while in college. Some parents express concern that a job could be an obstacle in making the transition to college or with the workload in general. Other parents believe that a job is not only financially necessary but it is important for the student to contribute financially to his education. Your family must decide both what is right and necessary to meet your child's and your family's obligations.

Student Loans

For most students, the financial aid package that is offered will also include some amount of loans, or money that will need to be repaid. **To learn the latest information about student loan programs and the most current options for your family, visit the Department of Education web site: www.studentaid.ed.gov.**

Understanding the Financial Aid Package

As mentioned earlier, once your child is accepted to a college, you will receive a financial aid package or award that outlines what kind and how much assistance your child can expect to receive. The important thing to remember about understanding the financial aid package is this: **If it's not in writing, it doesn't count. If you don't understand what is being offered, ASK!**

I have met with many families who accepted financial aid packages they did not understand and even rejected possible money because they did not realize what was being offered. There is no shame or embarrassment in needing to clarify the information you did – or did not – receive from a financial aid office.

Look in Appendix 9-B for a sample script of a phone call to the college's financial aid office to clarify or obtain needed information.

Remember: you are a valued customer of the college! When you call as a prospective "paying customer," you should expect to receive the help you need. As a parent, you are clearly concerned about your child's welfare. You want your child to receive every dollar of need-based and merit-based aid for which he is eligible. You need to understand clearly what is, and is not, being offered. So, do not be embarrassed to ask questions, and do not feel rushed in getting the information you need. If you need to take a day or two to visit the college financial aid office to understand financial aid options, please do this as soon as possible.

To help you keep track of any decisions or changes in your child's financial aid, **keep a file and notes of any conversations you have, the names of people you speak to or meet with as well as**

dates and times and file documents received from the financial aid office. Occasionally, you may need to make a written appeal about a financial aid decision, and your documentation of your conversations and written communications may be an essential paper trail to more effectively state your case.

College personnel sometimes use terms and speak of processes that are unfamiliar if you have not walked this path. **If you do not understand terms or concepts which they are sharing, ask for clarification.** And do not fool yourself into thinking you are the only parent out there who doesn't understand or who has questions. Some of America's wealthiest and most educated families hire consultants and coaches to navigate this journey with their child because they need assistance in this process too!

As mentioned earlier, finding the resources is often the most difficult part of this journey for you as parents. Whereas your child is most worried about getting accepted, you are often worried about having the money to pay for it. As adults, one of our worst fears is having to tell the child who worked hard to be accepted to the college of his dreams, "I'm sorry, but we cannot afford it."

Weighing the Costs

I know parents who have borrowed money way beyond their means to ensure their child achieved a college degree – something they were unable to do. Sometime this excessive borrowing strategy works. Other times, it does not. And the reality for many families is while they are struggling to pay for their child's college education, they are still fighting to keep food on the table at home.

One family's experience gave such a powerful reminder to me of how tough decisions can honor the child and the family. After working hard for many years, the daughter was accepted to an elite private university, a competitive state university, and the local community college. The daughter received a full ride to the community college, a substantial amount of aid to the state university, and all but $5000 from the more expensive private university.

After consulting with this family, the mother expressed concern that they were unclear about what was being offered by each school and what their family would have to pay in each case. So, I helped them set up a time to meet with a financial aid administrator at each school to explain the aid packages.

I felt confident that they would choose to attend the prestigious private school, because the student was very competitive academically and a real "go getter." However, the mother called to tell me that after much thought and family discussion, they decided that the child would attend the community college for the first two years and then transfer to a four year college later.

I was shocked and in fact speechless. I tried, diplomatically, to understand the family's pros and cons regarding the need to reject student loans altogether to attend two of the schools. But the mother's answer was very straightforward. She said, "We have been in debt all our lives, and we cannot afford to go into any more debt, no matter what. Community college may not be as prestigious, but it is free. We have other family needs too, including buying a car. So, we have talked about it as a family, and we have decided this is what is best for all of us – including my child. My child will live here at home and go to the community college, we will save money, and my child will be ready to go to a four year school in two years. I've cried, and I've prayed, and my child reassures me that this is the right thing to do."

Recently, I read in the paper that this young student was featured as an honors graduate from the community college and the recipient of many scholarships that will now pay for the remaining two years at the public university. Together, this family made their decision, the right decision for them. I admire them greatly for making the tough decisions, and they are, no doubt, an example for many others.

Involving Your Child

Every family will have to enter into similar dialogues about what is right for your child and your family. What is expensive for some will be a bargain for others – and vice versa. The right school at the right cost is a decision that must be made for each child at different times in the life of a family. Just remember: **Include your child in finding the resources, too.** Even though he may have never been a part of the financial decisions of the family, this is the time to introduce him to the costs of investing in his future. By doing so, you are preparing him more fully to send him on his way, not only to college, but to be prepared as a wise and faithful steward of the opportunities and money placed before him.

Chapter Nine Bright Ideas

1. Check out all potential financial aid options before ruling out any school because of money.

2. Document your "financial story" clearly – and quickly.

3. Check out the FAFSA web site for assistance in completing the FAFSA form in a timely manner.

4. Go to the web site www.fafsa4caster.ed.gov to get an early estimate of your family's eligibility.

5. Gather all the documents listed on the FAFSA checklist in Appendix 9-A before completing the FAFSA form.

6. Record and keep on file the secure codes for each college to which your child is applying.

7. Complete the FAFSA regardless of your family's income. You never know!

8. Check out your high school's past year's Awards Day program for possible scholarships.

9. Check out the web site www.studentaid.ed.gov for the latest information about student loan programs.

10. Ask questions and get clarity about what is specifically being offered in a financial aid package from any college. (Use the script in Appendix 9-B)

11. Keep documentation of all conversations regarding financial aid.

10

Sending Them on Their Way

Now the exciting work comes. Your child has been accepted to college. You have found or may still be finding the money to get him to college and keep him there. Now you need to get everything ready to send him on his way. Trying to remember what needs to be done between the fall and spring of the high school senior year when he is accepted to college and August when he leaves home can be overwhelming. So, let's look at several areas that need your consideration to help you and your child pave the way.

Room and Board

As a parent, you are obviously concerned about the roof over your child's head and the food on his table! Therefore, one of the first things you will need to address is where your child will live and where he will eat while attending college. Depending on the distance from home, some students choose to live at home and commute to school. Obviously, this eliminates the cost of campus housing and may reduce the cost of meals. However, other factors to be considered include travel costs to and from campus, parking, and the challenges of your child connecting in campus life.

Check with the college to see what housing options are available and what the school requires. Your child's college acceptance letter will often include instructions and time lines about deposits, orientation, housing, registration and requirements for incoming students. Some schools require students to live on campus their first year. Others allow off-campus housing for any students. Many schools strongly suggest that students live in a dorm the first few years as a means of easing the transition into college life. Granted, dorm living requires lots of adjustments for which your child needs to be aware such as crowded bathrooms, dealing with strange roommates, and lack of privacy. However, there are different options that are commonly available that you may want to discuss with your child.

Every college offers various housing options which may include single-sex dorms, coed dorms, substance-free dorms, singles, doubles, and suites. Colleges that offer single-sex dorms may also have associated visitation restrictions with guests of the opposite sex. Coed dorms also vary from school to school and even dorm to dorm, so **you may want to check what is meant by coed housing.** For instance, do girls and boys live on the same floor or different floors? Do they share a bathroom?

Some schools also offer chemical or substance-free dorms where students choose to live in an environment where alcohol, smoking and drug-use of any kind are not allowed. For many students, this removes both the temptation and the distraction that substance-use in the dorm can create. Another more recent option is special interest dorms such as international dorms or dorms for students with particular interests or majors.

Off-campus housing, such as apartments, are often not an option for first year students. However, you may begin conversations with your child about future housing options as he progresses through his years on campus. At this point, focus on that first year and the housing that will meet his needs now. You will need to help him decide the housing option that meets both his needs, values, and budget.

In addition to housing, **you also need to help your child determine which meal plan will best suit his needs and budget.** Meals plans vary from college to college from unlimited usage at any dining facility on campus including some off-campus dining options to a limited number of meals or credits per week or semester to be used. You should be receiving information from the college about the various dining and meal plan options shortly after your child has been accepted.

Packing 101

When your child moves off to college, he is essentially "setting up home" even if it is a really small home! So, when you begin making the "needs and wish" list for graduation presents, think compact! **Appendix 10-A offers a housing "essentials" checklist for items that your child may find helpful, if not essential,** as you begin to gather what he will need.

As mentioned earlier, think compact in size and storage space. Before you purchase or request items, your child may want to check with his future roommate to coordinate some purchases such as microwave, refrigerator or TV. Additionally, **check with the college to make sure that these items are allowed in the dorms.** Inevitably, you will probably forget something and will need to make that last minute trip to pick up forgotten supplies when you take your child to school. But at least this list will help you anticipate the most common needs.

School Supplies

For over twelve years now, you have been shopping for school supplies, but you are not done yet! In fact, the college school supply list may be longer than before since your child can no longer depend on the staples you have at home. **Appendix 10-B provides a school supplies checklist** to help you anticipate your child's needs away from home. Again, this list may not be all inclusive or may include items that are not necessary (or will be provided by the school). However, it is a spring board for deciding what is really needed.

One of the greatest supply expenses may be the computer needs of your child while at college. Many students use laptops for taking notes in lectures and for working on projects while away from their room. **Check with the college to see what is required or what is provided, such as student discounts for purchase of computers and wireless access on campus.**

Course Registration

Soon after being accepted to college, your child should receive information from the college about course registration. For incoming freshmen, many colleges want their first registration to be done in consultation with an advisor. Sometimes college placement tests are used to decide which courses your child should be enrolled in his freshman year. Therefore, your child may be asked to complete registration online requesting courses and alternates that will be reviewed, confirmed, or modified by his advisor. After completing this first step, he should receive a confirmed schedule for the fall. Often this schedule is confirmed during summer orientation.

Books

Another cost that often catches many students and families off guard that first year is books. In years past, students spent hours those first few days standing in line to purchase or rent text books. However, a new way to conserve money, time, and avoid undue stress is to purchase books ahead of time, possibly for a discount, online. Encourage your child to **get a list of the required texts for his courses ahead of time and rent or purchase books (used or new) online. Check out WithinViewWithinReach.com for current text purchasing guides.**

Of course, some students like to check out a class before purchasing textbooks. However, this "wait and see" approach may prevent your child from getting the books at a bargain, and if he waits too long, he may forget to read those required assignments!

Health Care

As a parent, you dread that first phone call when your child is sick and away from home. To prevent that "helpless" feeling for both of you, **check out what health care options are available on campus and off campus for your child.** Most colleges have student health centers that are well-equipped and experienced in responding to students' health care needs from immunizations to acute and chronic care. Many colleges may also offer some form of health care services for enrolled students. Additionally, you need to check on your current health insurance plan and what will or will not be covered for your child while he is enrolled in college.

To give you and your child a greater sense of comfort, while you are on campus during orientation or move in, you may want to go by the student health center to know where it is located, the hours, and how to access needed services.

Making Connections

Prior to your child's arrival on campus, he

will likely receive the contact information for his roommate. **Encourage your child to make roommate connections as early as possible** to begin dialogue and possibly even coordinate dorm room setup. Some students choose to coordinate together appliances, electronics, and even décor.

Communications

When your child leaves for college, you will probably want and need those regular times that you "touch bases." Granted, your need for communication with your child and your child's need, frequency, length, and type may differ from yours! So, **before your child leaves for campus, agree together on how and how often you will communicate.**

With the prevalence of cell phones and internet, most students either call, text or use their computer to call home instead of the old phone in the room much less a community phone down the hall! Access to communication may not be as big a challenge as the agreed upon timing. You and your child need to discuss how often and when he should call whether it's once a week, once a month, or only "as needed." The important thing to decide is what will meet both your need to stay connected and informed and your child's need to begin the journey of independence.

Money Management

As mentioned in earlier chapters, the college-bound process is often the first time that students have been actively involved in making major financial decisions. Likewise, living on their own on campus may be the first time your child is responsible for his daily finances.

Appendix 10-C includes a College Student Budget Worksheet. This worksheet helps you and your child anticipate what money will be available to him throughout the year from various income sources including scholarships, work, or a monthly stipend from you or others. The worksheet also helps your child plan for expenses including set costs (such as room and board or phone) as well as variable costs (such as entertainment or clothes). Some of the lines listed on the budget worksheet may not be applicable to your child's situation. However, it can be a springboard for developing your own worksheet based on anticipated income and expense line items.

Many families set up a student checking account that allows both you and your child access to the account. Most banks also offer online banking that will allow you to make deposits into your child's account online by transferring funds. How, when, and if you choose to use this service is dependent on both the capabilities and determination of each family.

The goal is to empower your child to make these financial choices on his own by planning ahead to make the money last throughout the year. What is important is helping your child to set a budget and to live by it. Inevitably, your child will encounter unexpected expenses. Additionally, many students experience at least once "running out" of money during that first year. You will need to decide ahead of time how you will respond to these "emergency" calls based on your own abilities, resources, and determination.

What is FERPA? And why does it matter?

FERPA stands for *Family Educational Rights and Privacy Act* and is a Federal law that protects the privacy of student education records. The reason it matters is each college and university has its own standard operating procedures regarding FERPA and how much information, if any, you can be provided about your child's academic or financial/billing records. **Get a clear understanding about these policies up front.** Whether your child attends a college on a "free ride" or whether mom and dad are footing the bill, **your college student will likely need to sign a release form for you to get any answers about his billing, payments or grades.**

Orientation/Welcome Day

Many colleges offer a welcome day prior to the beginning of classes for your child to take part in activities geared toward connecting them on campus and with other incoming students. These events offer fun-filled opportunities of varying interests but more importantly the opportunity for the students to get to know one another and the campus before classes begin. **Check the college acceptance packet and other mailings from the college for orientation and welcome day activities.**

Another benefit of being on campus before classes begin is to allow your child time to find the buildings where his classes will be held. This can eliminate the first day jitters and anxiety of not knowing where to go when!

Getting Them There... and Leaving Them There

Move-in day is inevitably an exciting and hectic day for all of you. Arriving on campus, you will find plenty of students, resident advisors (RAs), and others who will be there to greet and help. Take advantage of their capable hands and backs to get boxes unloaded.

Getting your child settled in his room may trigger a type of "nesting" response for some parents. I remember clearly my own experience of moving in my freshman year and the cleaning and sanitizing my mother did. It's amazing that we did not all die from the toxic fumes of all the various cleaners combined! I had actually witnessed the ritual with my mom when she took my aunt and uncles to college: sanitize, sanitize, anoint with oil!

You, likewise, may have the need to clean and organize your child's new "home." However, **be sensitive to this being your child's new home, not yours, and you might ask before you set up the room and offer to help.**

Once you have unpacked, answered any questions, gone over necessary forms, and helped your child have a sense of being "settled," it will soon be time for you to leave. It may be very tempting for you to linger as long as possible, but you need to allow him to start connecting on his own. As lonely as your child may seem, remember: He is surrounded by hundreds if not thousands of other freshmen who are "alone" for the first day, too.

There's No Place Like Home

One of the last questions often asked by parents as they prepare to leave their child at school is: "When will you be home?" Visits back home often depend on the student's course load, extra-curricular activities, social calendar, and budget. So, planning ahead for scheduled trips home may be difficult, but having the discussion will at least help set expectations on your part and your child's.

As part of the budgeting process, calculate the cost of travel between home and school, including mode of transportation: bus, car, train, or plane ticket. If your child has never been away from home for major celebrations or holidays, you will need to talk about which if any of these can be celebrated with family and how you might honor those occasions if he is away and unable to come home. Some scholarship programs will cover the cost of travel home for certain occasions, so make sure to check out this possibility, but do so at the beginning of the school year so you can anticipate what is or is not covered by other resources.

Within View, Within Reach

Because of distance, finances, or on-campus obligations, some students are able to return home only in the summers. Others are unable to return home their entire four years of school. This type of prolonged separation is usually very difficult for both the student and the family. So, if you anticipate this kind of separation may be necessary for your child, discuss this well in advance before pulling away from campus.

To anticipate when and how your child will come home, look at your child's academic calendar alongside your family's calendar to make homecoming plans. Once you have identified the anticipated trips, you can better respond to unanticipated or needed trips that emerge throughout the year. Proactive planning can help prevent unwanted tears – theirs and yours!

Return to Sender?

The first year of college is very exciting – and challenging – for every student. The year is filled with major adjustments for which you have attempted to prepare them. However, the best preparation (academic, social, emotional, physical, and spiritual) sometimes is not quite enough, and your child may not quite be ready for the pressures and experiences he might face. Additionally, despite your best efforts to find the right fit, your child may find that his current college home is not where he needs to be – at least for now.

So what happens if your child starts college and then finds that it is not right for him? High school seniors and their parents do not always have as much of the right information they need to make the best college selection. Additionally, situations and children change! The reality is that your child may conclude during that first year that the college where he is presently enrolled is not what will best serve him in the long run.

I am not in any way suggesting that your child go and "try out a college" for a year or less and then come home. As a parent, it is important to teach your child the importance of sticking with it, especially through the tough work and tough times. However, your child does need to know that you are willing to work with him if his experience goes beyond being merely tough to negative. When that happens, your child needs to know that you will be there to support him, even if it means bringing him back home for a brief time to reassess and reroute him to where he needs to be and to continue his growth.

Without a doubt, returning home after only a semester or a year of college can sting and even wipe out a child's confidence. As a result, it is often a "hush-hush" situation when a college student returns home. We need to let students know that while every decision has consequences, the decision to choose – and stay – with a particular college does not have to be an "end of the world" decision. **If your child needs to return home "for a season," this is not a failure on his part – or yours.** Use it as an opportunity to regroup and re-commission, applying what you have learned about who your child is and what he needs to grow and succeed.

Let your child know that you are open and want to talk about his experiences at college – even his struggles. Stay in touch with how he is doing, and affirm him along the way. Ask him about his support systems both on campus and off. And **allow him to succeed, and even fail, on his own, knowing that you will be there for him both in his successes and failures.**

Celebrating Their Right Next Steps

Congratulations, parents! You have brought them thus far on the journey. Now you have to let them go to try the next steps on their own. As when you let them take those first steps without your hands many years ago, you must let them try it now. Yes, they will stumble. They might even fall. They might get a few "'bumps and bruises" along the way. But it is all part of the journey. Of course, you will be there, watching and waiting in the wings, ready to pick them up when they fall and to reassure them when they hurt. Your work is not complete, but it is taking on a new form. So you, too, are learning the right next steps about how to walk along beside them, continuing to guide them, but from a different distance.

Your child will accomplish much with your capable guidance and others on the team. Over the next four or more years, you will need to continue helping him to see and believe what he is capable of becoming and doing, even in the midst of occasional disappointment and despair. So remember the words of wisdom with which we began this journey together:

Conceive it.

Believe it.

Achieve it.

Your child's future is *Within View*. It is *Within Reach*. Now help him go and get it!

Chapter Ten Bright Ideas

1. Check with the college to see what housing options are offered and required for incoming freshmen.

2. Determine which meal plan will best suit your child's needs and budget.

3. Look at Appendix 10-A for a Housing Essentials Checklist.

4. Check with the college (in the housing information) to determine which items are allowed and provided in the dorms.

5. Look at Appendix 10-B for a School Supplies Checklist.

6. Get a list of required texts ahead of time and rent or purchase new or used books online. Check out the book web site: www.withinviewwithinreach. com for links to text purchasing sites.

7. Check out health care options on campus and what your health insurance will cover.

8. Encourage your child to make roommate connections as early as possible.

9. Discuss and agree ahead of time how and how often you will communicate.

10. Look at Appendix 10-C for a College Student Budget Worksheet.

11. Find out about the college's FERPA policies and

have your child sign any necessary release forms.

12. Make plans to attend orientation and move-in day activities.

13. Be sensitive, when helping your child "settle in" that it is his new home – not yours.

14. Calculate and budget for travel home and set homecoming plans based on your child's and your calendars.

15. Encourage your child to talk openly and honestly about his college experiences and reassure him you will be there to support him in his successes and failures.

Appendices for Chapter 5

Finding the Right Fit

Appendix 5-A
Your Child's Best Learning Environment

1. What class size or structure does your child need to thrive?

2. Which teachers have been the most/least effective with your child and why?

3. Does he readily speak up and participate in class or does he tend to get "lost in the crowd" if so allowed?

4. How will he do being tossed into a much larger learning environment that requires him to be a self-starter?

5. Does he proactively seek help from teachers when he encounters problems with assignments or concepts?

6. How much "hand-holding" will your child require in a new learning environment or will he be able to figure it out from the start?

7. Does he like to be more "anonymous" or does he prefer a more intimate, relational setting where he likes being known and called on by name?

8. How much guidance does your child need in determining the right courses he needs to meet his academic or life goals?

9. Does your child perform better when he sets his own schedule and operates independently or when he is tracked and held accountable to complete tasks?

10. Would your child do better with an online degree to allow him to work at his own pace rather than follow a more structured, on-campus curriculum?

Appendix 5-B
How Your Child's School Compares with Others

1. How does your child's school or school system rank academic courses such as from most rigorous to the least rigorous. How does this compare with other schools in the area, state, nation?

2. To which colleges and universities did the high school's seniors: Apply? Get accepted? Enroll? Receive the most scholarship dollars?

3. How well do the school's teachers know and interact with each student?

4. What percentage of the high school's alumni have actually graduated from a four year college or university?

5. How involved is the school in helping students select and map out the best courses for their individual academic or life goals?

Appendix 5-C
Your Child's Level of Academic Challenge and Performance

1. What is your child's level of motivation as a student?

2. How hard is your child willing to work for "good" grades?

3. How many hours a night does your child spend doing homework?

4. How often does your child sacrifice other activities to excel on school projects?

5. How much does your child readily challenge himself in school?

6. Is your child taking the most rigorous courses he is capable of taking? If no, why not? Does your child pursue "high pressure" situations in academics or athletics?

7. Does your child thrive more in a competitive or cooperative setting?

8. Are there areas of study where your child struggles?

9. If so, will there be tutors available in the college setting to offer needed assistance?

10. Does your child like to read?

11. How will he handle the possible reading load required in certain academic settings?

12. Does your child like to write?

13. Does he feel threatened or intimidated when asked to write papers and how will he respond when having to write several papers at once?

14. How do your child's grades/grade point average compare to the average student admitted to certain colleges?

15. Compared with other students state-wide or nationally how do your child's scores on standardized tests (SAT, ACT) compare with the average scores of students admitted to certain colleges?

16. How well has your child performed in college-level courses (such as AP, IB, online, or community college courses)?

Appendix 5-D
Your Child's Social Needs

1. Does your child make friends easily?

2. Would he be able to find his "niche" on a larger campus of 20,000 or would he do better on a smaller campus of less than 2,000?

3. What does your child want in extracurricular activities including sports and other club activities?

4. Does your child want to participate competitively in sports during the college years?

5. Is your child ready for the diversity (ethnic, racial, religious, political) that will be found on certain college campuses?

6. Would your child adjust better living at home the first year or two to focus on the academic adjustments first?

7. What is your child's degree of maturity in being ready for the college transition?

Appendix 5-E
Questions to Ask the College

1. What is the size of the student body and the average class size for freshmen?

2. What major fields of study is the school known for and how do these match with your child's interests?

3. What specialty programs or schools are offered such as engineering, business, nursing, design?

4. Will there be sufficient extracurricular activities and structured social gatherings so that your child can get to know others and find where he belongs?

5. What does the school offer in extracurricular activities including sports and other club activities?

6. What graduate and post graduate programs does the school offer?

7. What networking opportunities are associated with this school?

8. What types of internship opportunities are available at this school?

9. What travel opportunities (including travel and study abroad) are offered by the school?

10. What recruitment opportunities does the school offer for graduating students?

11. What does the school offer in Residential Advising as well as tutorial and remedial academic

assistance?

12. What is the average score on standardized tests (SAT, ACT) of incoming freshmen?

13. What is the average GPA of incoming freshmen?

14. What is the male/female ratio of undergraduate students?

15. What percentage of the incoming freshmen actually graduate from the college?

16. What percentage of the students graduate in four years or in six years?

Appendices for Chapter 7

Appendix 7-A College Exploration

Exploration	Amount	
Campus Visits		
Gas		
Hotel		
Airline Tickets		
Food for travel		
Restaurant		
Tolls/Parking		
Souvenirs		
College Fairs		
Gas		
Parking		
Registration		
Application		
SAT, ACT test fees		
SAT, ACT prep courses		
AP/IB test fees		
Application Fees		
Express Shipping		
Total		

Appendix 7-B Cost Comparison Budget Worksheet
Expenses

School Name	College A	College B	College C
Tuition			
Fees			
Meal Plan			
Food			
Housing			
Books			
Transportation			
Personal Expenses			
Other			
Total			

Appendix 7-B Cost Comparison Budget Worksheet
Income

School Name	College A	College B	College C
Scholarships:			
College			
Church			
Local			
Other			
Grants			
Student Work Income			
Parents Contribution			
Loans			
Other			
Total			

Appendices for Chapter 9 Finding the Resources

Appendix 9-A
FAFSA Information Checklist from fafsa.ed.gov

1. Social security numbers for you, your spouse (if applicable) and your child who is the college-bound student.

2. Driver's license numbers for these same individuals (for those who have them).

3. The most current Federal Income Tax returns for you (and your spouse, if applicable) which may include:

- IRS 1040, 1040A, 1040EZ.
- Foreign Tax Return.

4. Your most recent untaxed income records which include:

- Veterans non-education benefit records.
- Child support received.
- Workers' compensation received.
- Your most current bank statements.

5. Your most current business and investment mortgage information, business and farm records, stocks, bonds, and other investment records.

6. Your alien registration or permanent resident card if you are not a US citizen.

Appendix 9-B
Sample Script for Phone Call
to Financial Aid Office

Hello, my name is _____, and I am calling on behalf of my child, _____, who has recently been accepted at _____.

I need some help understanding how much money you are offering and how much money we are expected to pay for him to enroll in August.

Is now an appropriate time, or should I make an appointment in the next few days for us to discuss this by phone or in person?

I really appreciate your help so we can resolve this in a timely fashion and so we can better understand our options and responsibilities.

Note:

Try to have hard copies of the Financial Aid award documents which have been sent to your child by the school.

Appendices for Chapter 10
Sending Them on Their Way

Appendix 10-A
Housing Essentials Checklist

	Twin bedding (comforter or bedspread, sheets, pillowcase, blanket)		Plastic food containers
			Ziploc bags
	Towel sets (bath towels and washcloths)		Small plastic tub (for washing dishes in sink)
			Dish cloth and towels
	Pillow(s)		Dish soap
	Twin mattress pad		Shower caddy
	Alarm clock radio		Soap
	Area rug(s)		Nail clippers
	Erasable message board		Mirror
	Corkboard and push pins		Hot/cold packs
	Wall calendar		Tissues
	Waste basket		Sewing kit
	Fan, if needed		Flashlight and batteries
	Posters/pictures		
	Compact storage bins (i.e. stacking or under bed)		First aid supplies (antibiotic ointment, adhesive bandages, hydrocortisone/anti-itch cream, pain reliever)
	Desk lamp		
	Potted plant		
	Clothes hamper		Extension cords
	Clothes hangers		Power strips
	Iron		
	Laundry supplies		
	Plastic dishes		

Appendix 10-B

College School Supplies Checklist

	Planner/Calendar		
	Calculator		
	Highlighters		
	Pens/pencils		
	Stapler		
	3-hole punch		
	USB drives		
	Backpack		
	Erasers		
	Binders		
	Index Cards		
	Notebooks		

Appendix 10-C
College Student Budget Worksheet

	Amount			Amount
Monthly Expenses			**Monthly Income**	
Rent/Housing			Work	
Cell Phone			Parents	
Utilities			Financial Aid	
Groceries			Other	
Eating Out			**Subtotal**	
Entertainment				
Car Expenses			Yearly Income	
Transportation			Scholarships	
Laundry			Financial Aid	
Personal Expenses			Other	
Credit Cards			**Subtotal**	
Miscellaneous			Total Income	
Other			Total Income	
Subtotal			– Total Expenses	
			Difference	
Yearly Expenses				
Tuition				
Student Fees				
Other Fees				
Books				
Total				

About The Book: *Within View, Within Reach*

More than twenty-five years after being offered admission and full scholarships to Duke University, Harvard University and the University of North Carolina at Chapel Hill, Robyn S. Hadley continues to assist students, families and others in the process of navigating the college-bound journey.

Based on her own personal experiences as well as the experiences of many students and families she has helped over the years, *Within View WIthin Reach* gives the reader a complete picture of the kinds of things parents and their teenagers need to think about during high school. This also includes the process of considering colleges and applying for college, financial aid and scholarships.

Within View, Within Reach is a "How To" guide for parents that educates them about the world of college admissions and how they can best assist their teenager in finding the right college and paying for it. In this book, Hadley shares a roadmap for parents to assist their teenager in navigating the college bound journey and how to bring the dream of a college education from *Within View to Within Reach.*

About the Author

A product of small town America: Graham, North Carolina, Robyn S. Hadley was educated in the public schools of Alamance County and went on to receive a Morehead Scholarship to UNC-Chapel Hill and a Rhodes Scholarship to Oxford University in 1985.

Since college, Hadley has helped teenagers and parents understand how to prepare for college and pay for it. Her work in this area had been mostly as a volunteer until 2004 when she made a career change and started a non-profit, college preparatory program, YESICAN, for children in her hometown. From there, she began consulting in the field of college access and for the past five years has served the Alamance-Burlington School System in North Carolina as Founder and Executive Director of The "What's After High School?" Program.

The book, *Within View, Within Reach* is the first in a series which brings together the proven advice and instructions Hadley has provided to teenagers and parents over the years resulting in college admissions, undergraduate and graduate degrees, financial aid and scholarship dollars, successful interviews, travel abroad opportunities, internships in the US and abroad and finally jobs!

Youth Enrichment Series, Inc.

Started in 2004, Y.E.S. I CAN Program is a faith-based, college preparatory program for students in grades 3-12 and their families. The program is produced by Youth Enrichment Series, Inc., staffed by volunteers and focuses on teaching children how to develop and execute faith-based life skills for being successful in the 21st century. Outcomes include:

- graduating from high school
- pursuing higher education and/or technical training and financial aid to pay for it
- becoming gainfully employed
- adopting healthy lifestyles

Programming for parents, guardians and family members teaches them how to identify and utilize available resources that will help in assisting their children excel in school, get a college degree, pay for college and get a job! Youth Enrichment Series, Inc. was established in 2007 and is a 501(c)(3) organization.

P.O. Box 843
Graham, NC 27253
www.yeseries.org
Telephone: 336-228-0234

For More Information

For updated college information, checklists and guides you can download, please visit our website:

www.withinviewwithinreach.com

Corporate sponsorship opportunities and bulk orders are available.
Please contact us through the website.

Within View Within Reach:
Navigating the College-Bound Journey
by Robyn S. Hadley

Published by
Samuel Stone Press
Post Office Box 974 • Graham, North Carolina 27253
www.samuelstonepress.com